YOUTH UNEMPLOYMENT

By the same author

Introduction to Mathematical Economics
The Future of the Multinational Enterprise (*with Peter J. Buckley*)
Alternatives to the Multinational Enterprise

YOUTH UNEMPLOYMENT

Mark Casson

First published 1979 by
THE MACMILLAN PRESS LTD
London and Basingstoke
Associated companies in Delhi
Dublin Hong Kong Johannesburg Lagos
Melbourne New York Singapore Tokyo

British Library Cataloguing in Publication Data

Casson, Mark
    Youth unemployment
    1. Youth – Employment – Great Britain
    2. Unemployed – Great Britain
    I. Title
    331.3'4   HD6276.G7

ISBN 978-0-333-26565-9   ISBN 978-1-349-16120-1 (eBook)
DOI 10.1007/978-1-349-16120-1

For Helen Hudson

Contents

List of Tables
and Figures

FIGURES

Acknowledgements

My interest in the problem of youth unemployment began when I was invited to prepare a report on the subject for the Directorate General of Employment and Social Affairs of the Commission of the European Communities. On their initiative an approach was made to the Directorate of Social and Demographic Statistics of the Statistical Office of the European Communities for permission to use unpublished tabulations from the biennial Labour Force Sample Survey. I should like to thank the Commission for financial support in preparing the original report, and also acknowledge the help received from the Statistical Office, both in preparing the report and in producing the present work. I cannot name the individuals concerned, but nevertheless I am very grateful to them. Needless to say, neither the Commission nor the Statistical Office necessarily concurs either with the analysis and interpretation of the evidence, nor with the views on policy expressed in this book.

The manuscript has benefited considerably from the comments and criticisms of Paul Cheshire, John Creedy, Geoffrey Denton, Peter Hart, Ros Ingham, David Metcalf and Richard Pankhurst. Naturally the responsibility for all errors and omissions is mine alone.

Special thanks are due to Gerard Dummett, who gave up part of his summer vacation to help in the preparation of the statistical tables which appear in the text.

The manuscript was typed most efficiently by Barbara Wall, Joan Horton, Margaret Lewis, Maggie Fillingham and Cynthia Fido. Once again I must thank my wife for looking after the interests of the non-specialist reader.

M. C. C.

1 Introduction

1.1 SCOPE OF THE STUDY

This book aims to answer three major questions.

(1) Why is the rate of unemployment persistently higher among young people than among most other age groups?
(2) Why has youth unemployment increased so dramatically in the current world recession? More generally, why is youth unemployment particularly sensitive to cyclical fluctuations in aggregate demand, so that it increases faster than average in a recession and recovers more quickly in a reflation?
(3) What explains the rising postwar trend in youth unemployment, which has been apparent in most industrial countries?

An examination of these questions leads to a discussion of the following policy issues:

(1) To what extent is the high rate of unemployment among young people associated with special problems of entry into working life? Can such problems be mitigated by structural changes in the youth labour market? If so, what is the appropriate long-term strategy for implementing these changes?
(2) Is it possible to reduce youth unemployment in the short term without increasing unemployment among other age groups? If so, can a policy of employment creation be devised which is not inflationary?
(3) Is the capacity of industrial society to offer worthwhile employment to young people on the decline? Are young people becoming increasingly uncompetitive in relation to other groups of workers? If so, can the situation be remedied by institutional changes – for example, by a closer integration of education and industry? Or must future social policy be based on the assumption that increasing unemployment among young people is inevitable?

1

This study exploits new and invaluable statistical evidence generated by the biennial EEC Labour Force Sample Survey, details of which are given in the Appendix. The analysis of the statistics is a comparative one. The behaviour of young workers is compared with that of workers in other age groups; it is also compared across countries, and at different points in time. The study focuses on three countries – West Germany, Italy and the United Kingdom – using data for 1973 and 1975. It would have been possible to cover more countries, but in a work of this nature a detailed examination of a small number of cases is more productive than a superficial examination of a large number of cases. The three particular countries were chosen because they apparently differ very much as regards the nature and magnitude of their youth unemployment. Thus, taken together the experiences of these countries provide a strong test of any general theory of youth unemployment. The empirical analysis makes it possible to assess the relative importance of various causes of youth unemployment and the extent to which the influences on youth unemployment vary from one country to another.

1.2 DEFINITION AND MEASUREMENT OF YOUTH UNEMPLOYMENT

For the purposes of this study 'youth' is defined as the age group fourteen to twenty-four inclusive, with a further distinction between teenagers, i.e. those aged fourteen to nineteen inclusive, and young adults, aged twenty to twenty-four. These classifications correspond to those used by the Statistical Office of the European Communities, but not necessarily to those used by the member states of the EEC.

An unemployed person may be defined as someone without employment who is actively seeking a job of a certain specification and would be willing to accept such a job if it were offered at the prevailing money wage; the type of job referred to is normally a regular full-time employment. It is important to distinguish between an unemployed person and a job-seeker. Job-seekers include people outside the working population – those undertaking education or military service, doing housework, and so on – who wish to enter employment, and those in employment who are mismatched to their jobs and are seeking more suitable work. Job-seekers who are not unemployed may nevertheless represent a kind of concealed unemployment – people who have taken a 'second-best' role, because the jobs to which they are most suited are unavailable.

The concepts of unemployment and job search outlined above harmonise quite well with the concepts used in the EEC Labour Force Sample Survey (see the Appendix). However, there is a considerable difference between this concept of unemployment and the concept used by member states in the compilation of their national series on unemployment. Most national series count a person as unemployed only if he is registered as such with a local labour office. It is generally believed that many young people, particularly teenagers, do not register, because they are too young to be eligible for benefits, or because they do not consider it worth their while given the scarcity of suitable jobs.[1] Comparisons of unemployment between age groups may be complicated by other biases in registration: for example, older workers who are not actively seeking work and who may never work again may continue to register as unemployed to qualify for higher pensions. Thus, a comparison of unemployment rates for young and old using national series could be highly misleading, as the registration figures will tend to understate unemployment among the young and overstate unemployment among the old.

1.3 THE SOCIAL SIGNIFICANCE OF YOUTH UNEMPLOYMENT

Unemployment of any kind represents a potential wastage of resources. But there are special reasons why unemployment among young people is likely to have enduring economic and social consequences.[2]

It has been argued that the period immediately following entry into working life exerts a strong influence on subsequent attitudes to employment. Prolonged unemployment can lead to resentment directed not only against specific employers who have rejected job applications, but also against employers in general. As a result firms will find that, in later life, the worker appears lacking in motivation, and is uncooperative or even disruptive.

Workers' discontent may also extend to the political sphere. In the early 1930s, in the middle of the Great Depression, there was anxiety lest high rates of unemployment among the young lead to political violence, or even revolution. The danger was associated not only with unskilled workers who were unemployed, but also with young intellectuals who were forced to take jobs well below their aspirations. On this view, any society with an instinct for self-preservation must take young people's reactions to unemployment very seriously.

Youth is the period when people are best able to benefit from training. Their adaptability makes it easy for them to grasp new ideas and learn techniques quickly. If training is postponed until the worker is older, it is likely to take longer for the same proficiency to be achieved. Furthermore, when training for a career, the period over which the training costs are paid back is shorter the later the training is completed.

Most skilled jobs require a period of 'on-the-job' training. In a recession a contraction of vacancies for skilled workers means that many young people must postpone their training until the recovery begins. If the recession is a long one, employers may prefer to take more of the new generation of young workers rather than recruit unemployed members of the previous generation. Although on average the older workers will be more able, their suitability for training and their 'pay-back' period will have declined. Thus, the older generation will miss out on their training opportunities. This not only reduces the quality of the skilled labour force of the future, but also creates inequality of opportunity between different generations of young people.

Finally, unemployment gives young workers plenty of idle time. This time can be spent usefully – searching for jobs, undertaking voluntary services, and so on; but more often it is spent either in the home or on the streets. Staying at home can build up tensions in the family, particularly where some members are working and others are unemployed. For this reason many young people prefer to spend their time on the streets, while some of the older ones leave home altogether. In either case, it has been suggested, there is a danger that young people will become involved in small-time crime. Criminal pursuits provide casual work with tax-free income, and can often be rationalised in terms of grievances against a society which has no employment to offer.

The discussion above highlights some of the possible long-term consequences of youth unemployment. It does not seek to minimise the problems of unemployment among other age groups. But it can be argued that, in the past, society has placed too much reliance on the adaptability and resilience of youth. The employment problems of young workers are inextricably linked with the employment problems of the aging workers of the same generation at a later date. Thus the study of youth unemployment not only is important in its own right, but also sheds light on the problem of unemployment in the workforce as a whole.

1.4 SUMMARY OF RECENT STATISTICAL EVIDENCE

A relatively high incidence of unemployment among young workers has persisted for some considerable time in most EEC countries.[3] Table 1.1 shows how the rate of unemployment varied with respect to age in West Germany, Italy and the UK in 1973 and 1975. The figures for West Germany must be treated with some caution, since they do not cover foreign guest workers living in hostels; there is evidence that unemployment rates among these workers are higher than among workers living in private households, so that over all the figures may understate rates of unemployment in West Germany.

For each country, and for both sexes, the highest rate of unemployment is recorded in the fourteen to nineteen age group. Thereafter it tends to decline steadily with age, although the decline is more noticeable among men than among women. Unemployment does not

TABLE 1.1 Percentage unemployment by selected age groups, 1973 and 1975

| | Age group | | | | |
	14–19	*20–24*	*25–29*	*30–34*	*All ages*
1973					
Men					
Italy	18·8	12·3	4·8	1·4	3·3
UK	4·5	3·2	2·1	2·3	2·4
W. Germany	1·2	0·6	0·3	0·3	0·4
Women					
Italy	18·7	13·2	7·6	3·2	6·1
UK	2·9	2·4	2·4	2·5	1·7
W. Germany	1·4	0·7	0·9	0·6	0·8
1975					
Men					
Italy	15·2	10·7	4·2	1·4	2·7
UK	8·8	7·1	4·1	3·5	4·2
W. Germany	6·3	5·1	3·8	2·6	2·8
Women					
Italy	17·0	12·2	5·5	2·2	4·9
UK	9·3	6·9	8·1	7·1	5·2
W. Germany	6·7	3·7	3·3	3·4	3·2

Source: European Labour Force Sample Survey 1973 and 1975.

increase systematically until retiring age is approached, and even then it is significantly lower than among the young. Differences in youth unemployment between men and women tend to reflect differences in the working population as a whole: unemployment tends to be marginally higher among women than among men.

In recent years there has been a discernible trend for the proportion of young workers among the unemployed to increase. Figure 1.1 presents logarithmic plots of the number of young workers registered as unemployed in Germany, Italy and the UK for the period 1966–77. It can be seen that for each country there is a tendency for the gap between

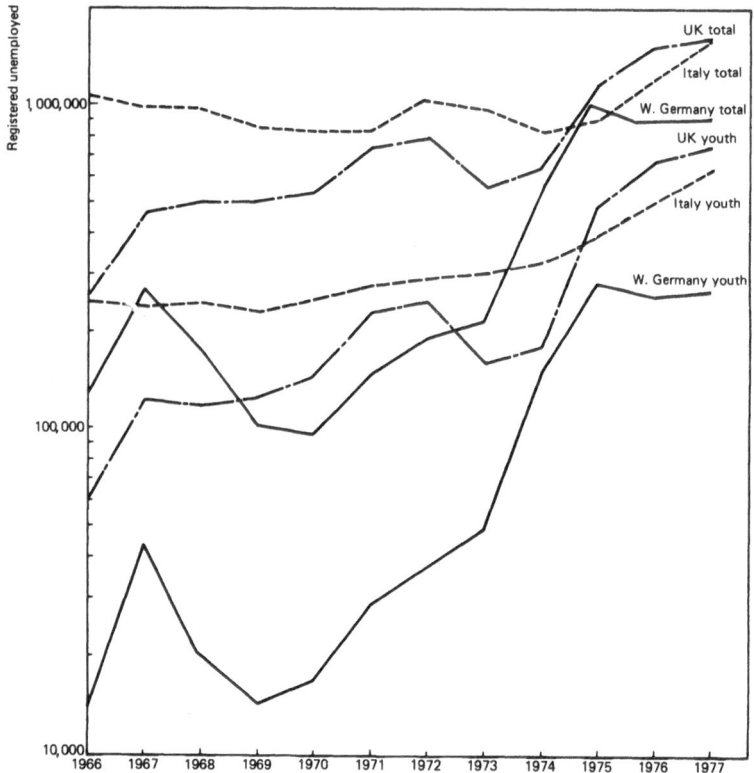

Source: EEC summary statistics.

FIGURE 1.1   Youth unemployment and total unemployment in W. Germany, Italy and the UK, 1966–77

the graph of youth unemployment and the graph of total unemployment to narrow over time; since the graph is logarithmic this means that
the proportion of young workers among the unemployed has tended to
increase. Demographic factors such as the changing age distribution of
the working population may account for part of this tendency, but it is
unlikely that this is the complete explanation.

The graphs for West Germany and the UK also show that the
fluctuations in youth unemployment are exaggerated compared with
the fluctuations in total unemployment. Youth unemployment and total
unemployment have the same frequency and vary in step with one
another, but the amplitude of the fluctuations in youth unemployment
is much greater.[4] In Italy levels of unemployment are much higher and,
if anything, youth unemployment fluctuates less than does total
unemployment, though both series are relatively stable.

1.5 PLAN OF THE BOOK

Chapter 2 reviews previous studies of youth unemployment, and sets
the subject in a broad social context. It considers the influence of
education, family background, residential area and occupational preferences on the type of work taken by young people, the number of job
changes they experience, and the consistency with which they follow a
chosen career. It is shown that in a number of fundamental respects the
character of the youth labour market has changed little since youth
unemployment was first studied, over seventy years ago.

Chapter 3 reviews recent advances in the theory of the labour market,
and develops their implications for the analysis of unemployment.
Particular emphasis is placed on the role of job search in unemployment. The significance of this analysis for youth unemployment is
examined in Chapter 4. A number of theories are presented, each
designed to explain some aspect of unemployment among young
people.

The results of the EEC Labour Force Sample Survey are discussed in
Chapter 5. In Chapter 6 the statistical evidence is used to test alternative
theories of youth unemployment.

Chapter 7 reviews policies for reducing youth unemployment. Each
policy is evaluated in the light of the preceding analysis. It is argued that
in the future more care must be exercised in the design of short-term job-
creation programmes. There are several long-term measures which
could be introduced to improve the efficiency of the youth labour

market. Among other things, these measures would reduce 'frictional' unemployment among young workers. It is suggested that topical interest in the specific problem of unemployed school-leavers has diverted attention from more fundamental problems, the solution of which requires radical changes in the youth labour market.

2 Youth Unemployment in Historical Context

2.1 INTRODUCTION

This chapter offers an historical perspective on youth unemployment. It reviews the origins of the study of youth unemployment and traces developments in the UK since the turn of the century. As such, it fills a gap in existing literature by providing a critical appraisal of earlier works on the subject.[1] More significantly, it demonstrates that the characteristics of youth unemployment have changed little in the seventy years that have elapsed since the subject was first seriously investigated.

2.2 THE BOY-LABOUR PROBLEM

A major social issue of the late Victorian period was the use of juvenile labour – principally boys – in casual and unskilled occupations: the so-called 'boy-labour problem'.[2] It was believed that there was an excess demand for juvenile labour in certain 'blind-alley' occupations. Juveniles were recruited straight from school and discharged after two or three years, without having received any training, to swell the 'reserve army' of unskilled labour, while their place was taken by a new generation of school-leavers.

Unemployment among the very young (fourteen- to seventeen-year-olds) was not considered a problem: the difficulty arose in connection with the transition to more secure and skilled employment in the late 'teens. According to Beveridge,

> it is clear that a great many boys and girls on leaving school enter occupations in which they cannot hope to remain for more than a few years and in which they are not being fitted for any permanent career. With the . . . development of trades and processes to which appren-

9

ticeship has never been applied, there has come a break-up in the
continuity of industrial life. The principle of apprenticeship was that
people should enter in early youth the craft in which they would
remain to the end. At the present time . . . some [industries] use far
more boys than they can possibly find room for as men. . . . They are
the 'blind-alley' occupations which have to be abandoned when
man's estate is reached. . . . [The boys] enter, not as learners, but
as wage earners, doing some work too simple or too light to require
the services of grown people. When, therefore, they themselves grow
up and begin to expect the wages of grown people, they must go
elsewhere to obtain these wages. They leave or are dismissed and their
places are taken by a fresh generation from the schools. They find
themselves at eighteen or twenty without any obvious career before
them, without a trade in their hands, and with no resources save
unskilled labour. They go therefore – very likely after a period of
military service – to overcrowd that already crowded market.[3]

A number of blind-alley occupations were identified in a survey
reported by Tawney.[4] The classic case was that of van-boy, but there
were many other trades in which the boys employed far outnumbered
the positions available for men, as Table 2.1 shows. In biscuit-making,
finishing, soap-making and weaving, for example, the boys employed
outnumber the men, although for a completely even age distribution

TABLE 2.1   Employment of men and boys in various establishments, c. 1909

Establishment or activity	Men	Boys	Ratio of boys to men
Biscuit-making	12	41	3·4
Finishing company – raising	10	18	1·8
Soap-making	98	114	1·2
Weaving	120	126	1·1
Finishing company – storemills	40	40	1·0
Finishing company – drying	28	26	0·9
Sawmills – machine shop	78	64	0·8
Sawmills – chair shop	38	14	0·4
Sawmills – turning	30	4	0·1
Pastry-making	60	7	0·1
Finishing company – pressing	96	10	0·1
Bread-making	96	8	0·1

Source: R. H. Tawney, 'Economics of Boy Labour', *Economic Journal*, 19
(1909) 517–37. Reproduced by permission of Cambridge University Press.

there would be need to be at least six men to every boy.[5] It is evident that in these industries the openings for young adults were far fewer than the number of young workers eligible for them.

This in itself is not an evil, provided that the young workers receive suitable training to equip them for transition to adult work in other trades. However, Tawney argues that, where training was provided, it was usually far too specialised. Many apprentices were in fact no more than specialised machine-minders; they learnt only one branch of the trade, and soon lost the ability to adapt to other work. In any case, many young people did not stay in jobs long enough to acquire any training at all.[6] Like many other writers of the period, Tawney concluded that the poor quality of training, coupled with the excessive mobility of young workers, was wasting away what he regarded as the nation's principal asset – namely, the young people who constitute the workforce of the future.

2.3   PRE-1914 SOCIAL SURVEYS

It was something of a surprise when the early social surveys of juvenile labour revealed a significant unemployment problem among young people. Using the survey techniques pioneered by Charles Booth, Rowntree and Lasker conducted an investigation into unemployment in York in June 1910.[7] All working-class households were visited, and personal details of the unemployed collected. It was discovered that 'a surprisingly large number' of youths were not only without work, but had been without it for a considerable time. In fact, of the 129 youths aged fourteen to eighteen inclusive that were interviewed, seven had been unemployed for over one year and sixteen for over six months.

Rowntree and Lasker noted four main characteristics of the young unemployed. The first was their poor educational attainments. Although 66 per cent of school-leavers in York attained the seventh standard in 1910, only 31 per cent of the unemployed had reached this level. Secondly, the unemployed were typically of low intelligence, physically weak or disabled, and came from unsatisfactory homes. It was estimated that 80 per cent of the unemployed were disadvantaged in one or other of these ways. Thirdly, their previous employment was largely unskilled or casual or both: 42 per cent were first employed as errand boys, while only 2 per cent had taken apprenticeships. Finally, most of the youths changed jobs frequently. They appeared to favour short periods of work in dead-end jobs with intervening periods of unemployment – 'usually spent in the streets, where they pick up odd jobs'.

A typical case history is that of a boy who left school at fourteen to become an errand boy for a shop.

In a few months he left, and after being out of work for nine weeks, was engaged as a page boy. In this situation again, he stayed only for a year or so, and left of his own accord to learn French polishing. At this occupation he earned seven shillings a week, but had to be dismissed after ten months because he did not give satisfaction. . . . Since then he has obtained temporary work as an errand boy earning 5s. 6d. a week, and since the inquiry was made has been at an engine works at a wage of ten shillings a week.

Rowntree and Lasker remark that 'it is obvious that such frequent changes make for general instability. Taking into account periods of unemployment, probably a permanent occupation at a lower wage would have yielded a better financial result than this constant change with occasional short periods of relatively high wages; as well as being morally more desirable'.[8]

It was Rowntree and Lasker's belief that many of the problems of unemployment generally stem from unsatisfactory experiences of entry into working life. Recurrent exposure to unemployment when young can stimulate a taste for idleness, and provide an introduction to small-time criminal pursuits. Furthermore, many of the best jobs – such as apprenticeships – are offered only to school-leavers, so that, once he is unemployed, a young worker's prospects may be considerably reduced.

The significance of frequent job-changing among young people was a theme developed by Freeman, in a study published three years later.[9] He examined a sample of seventy-one fourteen-year-old boys who left school in Birmingham in 1909. The study was confined to chronic job-changers – those who had taken four or more jobs in the three years since leaving school. The boys were classified into three categories, according to whether they were destined for skilled work (class I), for unskilled work (class II), or to become unemployable through physical, mental or moral defect (class III). The classification was made twice: once at fourteen years of age, on the basis of teacher's reports, and once at seventeen, on the basis of a series of interviews. The results are summarised in Table 2.2.

Although there is a strong subjective element in Freeman's classification, his results clearly indicate the deteriorating prospects of the

TABLE 2.2   Mobility of a sample of young workers in Birmingham, 1909–12

Destined class of work at 14	Destined class of work at 17			
	I	*II*	*III*	*Total*
I	6	13	–	19
II	–	31	4	35
III	–	–	17	17
All classes	6	44	21	71

Source: A. Freeman, *Boy Life and Labour: The Manufacture of Inefficiency* (London: P. S. King & Son, 1914), Chs 2–4.

Note: Classes as explained in text.

chronic job changers: nineteen of the fourteen-year-olds appeared destined for skilled work, but only six of the seventeen-year-olds, while twenty-one of the seventeen-year-olds appeared destined to be unemployable, four more than among the fourteen-year-olds. Not surprisingly, the reasons for job-changing varied considerably as between those who finished up in class I and those who finished up in class III. Most of those in class I changed because of the limited experience they were gaining of their chosen trade, and changed to other jobs within the same trade, in order to broaden their experience. On the other hand, some of those in class III could scarcely remember the previous jobs they had had, and appeared to be constantly on the look-out for what they regarded as easy ways of making money.

2.4   YOUTH UNEMPLOYMENT IN THE GREAT DEPRESSION

When the world economy entered recession in the late 1920s it soon became apparent that the employment prospects of school-leavers were very poor, and by the early 1930s there were a large number of youngsters who had not had the opportunity of a steady job for several years. There was considerable concern about the demoralisation that this situation produced among the young unemployed, and anxiety lest the frustration lead to political unrest.

The first major study during the Depression was by Jewkes and Winterbottom,[10] who carried out a survey of 21,000 school-leavers in

Lancashire in the autumn of 1932. They recorded the duration of unemployment among school-leavers, and their occupational choice. In view of the depressed state of the economy and the declining international competitiveness of the cotton industry – the staple industry of the area – it is not surprising that the duration of unemployment tended to be fairly high. Certain features of the juvenile labour market had changed little since before the war. In particular, employment among fourteen- and fifteen-year-olds was much higher than among older children. Approximately 80 per cent of fourteen-year-old school-leavers obtained placements within three months. Most of these placements were in the cotton industry and retail distribution, where long-term employment prospects were very poor. Workers in the cotton industry tended to be discharged before their sixteenth birthday, when the employer began to pay unemployment and health-insurance contributions; consequently unemployment among sixteen-year-olds was particularly high. In retailing, wages were low and many left the industry voluntarily. The low demand for sixteen-year-olds led to the paradox that children who had the longest education were least able to obtain employment.

The most important study of youth unemployment in the interwar period was by Cameron, Lush and Meara.[11] They surveyed 1561 young men aged eighteen to twenty-five who were registered as unemployed in the summer of 1937. The survey involved a 10 per cent sample of the young unemployed in three urban areas: Glasgow, Liverpool and Cardiff. The employment history of each youth was recorded from his leaving school until the outbreak of war in 1939. At the time the national unemployment rate for this age group averaged about 15 per cent.

Two facts were immediately apparent. First, the incidence of unemployment increased with age. The proportion of the three-year period spent unemployed rose steadily from about 10 per cent at age fifteen to a peak of about 24 per cent at age twenty-two. Unemployment at fourteen was slightly higher than at fifteen, while from twenty-two onwards it began to decline slowly. Secondly, the incidence of unemployment was very unequal. The 20 per cent of youths most prone to unemployment spent four times as long on the dole as did the 14 per cent least prone to unemployment. For each youth the past history of unemployment was a very good guide to his present employment status.

Contrary to Jewkes and Winterbottom, Cameron *et al.* found that the incidence of unemployment was much lower the later the youth had left school. This effect did not significantly diminish with age. Among those who were married, chronic unemployment (no more than six months' employment in three years) was much more common. Part of the explanation may be the much higher rate of unemployment allowance paid to married and family men: half the unemployed married men were receiving an unemployment allowance equalling or exceeding the weekly wage in their last job. Moreover, any employment they were likely to find at a higher wage would probably be casual, seasonal or prone to unexpected stoppages, all of which would increase the unpredictability of the income. It appears that, because of the difficulties of household budgeting, many wives had a definite preference for the steady income yielded by the state allowance as opposed to the fluctuating income generated by private employment.

Cameron *et al.* place considerable emphasis on the role of personal appearance in securing work: the chronically unemployed tended to be shorter, lighter and less well dressed than the others. However, it proved difficult to distinguish cause and effect: were shortness and lightness the result of the poor diet of the unemployed and their poor dress a reflection of their inability to afford new clothes, or was their appearance a cause of their being refused work?

A common grievance among the unemployed was that only inferior jobs were to be found through the Employment Exchange. It is certainly true that fewer than 20 per cent of all jobs were found through official agencies (see Table 2.3). It was a widespread belief among the youths that the best jobs were obtained through 'influence' – which could mean a recommendation from an employer's major customer, or merely being on good terms with the foreman. Very few of the youths were trade-

TABLE 2.3   Methods of obtaining jobs, 1937

Age group	No. of jobs	Percentage of jobs obtained through				
		own efforts	relatives and friends	official agencies	other means	Total
14–17	2607	62·6	18·0	18·7	0·7	100·0
18 +	3523	69·9	10·7	18·6	0·8	100·0
Both groups	6130	66·8	13·8	18·7	0·7	100·0

Source: C. Cameron, A. Lush and G. Meara, *Disinherited Youth: A Report on the 18 +Age Group Enquiry Prepared for the Trustees of the Carnegie United Kingdom Trust* (Edinburgh: T. and A. Constable, 1943), Table 27.

union members and trade-union contacts were of little help in obtaining placement.

The type of work obtained varied considerably according to age. The distributive trades were major employers: they accounted for 39 per cent of all jobs for fourteen- to sixteen-year-olds, falling to 18 per cent of jobs for those aged twenty-one and over. The very large entry into distribution may be partly accounted for by the relative growth of this sector of the economy in the 1930s (owing, for example, to the switch from rail to road transport). Nevertheless, the skewness of the age distribution in the distributive trades implies a very high turnover of young workers. Reasons given for leaving jobs also varied considerably according to age (Table 2.4). The under-eighteens were much more likely to quit; and in cases where they were dismissed it was more likely to be because they had become too old, or because they were unsuitable for the work. Straightforward redundancy was much less common than it was for the eighteen-plus age group.

Most young men were dissatisfied with the wages offered to them, relative to older groups. They resented being recruited as 'cheap labour' and being asked to continue at juvenile rates when they came of age. In some cases young workers who had refused to continue at juvenile rates had been made redundant, and many young workers left their jobs after arguments over whether the employer should pay them the same wage as the older worker they had displaced. It seems that the resistance to competitive pressures was sufficient to maintain considerable inequality of earnings with respect to age.[12] The twenty-four-year-olds, when employed, received on average five times as much as fourteen-year-olds; the main discontinuities in pay scales were at sixteen, eighteen and twenty-one. It is not surprising that, with such inequalities, major reasons for redundancy were 'too old at sixteen', 'too old at eighteen' and 'too old at twenty-one'.

Corroboration of many of these findings is provided by an earlier study, by Jewkes and Jewkes.[13] They surveyed 2038 young people who left elementary schools in five Lancashire towns at Easter 1934.

About one-half of the school-leavers changed jobs once or more during the first two years of working life, while one-fifth changed jobs twice or more. The frequency of job-changing fell over time, but there remained significant differences between occupations. Turnover was generally highest in retailing, except in one town: in this case there was a relative shortage of labour, wages were high in retailing, and turnover was negligible.

Unlike many other studies, this one obtained considerable success in

TABLE 2.4 Reasons for leaving job, 1937

Age group	Total no. of jobs	Work finished	Firm closed down	Paid off owing to age	Wages too low	No prospects, disliked job, etc.	Illness or accident	Dismissed as unsuitable	Total
						Reason job left (%)			
14–17	1926	36·8	8·9	18·5	10·8	11·6	5·2	8·2	100·0
18 +	3388	71·8	3·3	6·0	5·3	4·1	4·2	5·3	100·0
Both groups	5314	59·2	5·5	10·5	7·1	6·8	4·6	6·3	100·0

Source: Cameron, Lush and Meara, *op. cit.*, Table 28.

following the careers of those who left the district during the period of the survey. Most of the migrants moved along with their families, and in general were successful in obtaining more stable and higher-paid jobs. The authors noted considerable differences in employment prospects in neighbouring towns, which pointed to significant economic gains to migration. However, it appeared that few young people were willing or able to live away from their families, and transport costs were sufficiently high relative to juvenile wages to discourage all but very short-distance commuting.

2.5 EARLY POSTWAR STUDIES

In the early postwar period increasing attention was paid to young people's transition from school to work. There were several studies concerned with broad social issues such as education, delinquency and the social development of the adolescent. This reflects the preoccupation of policy at that time with extending education and creating equality of opportunity within a full-employment society.

A few of these studies produced important evidence on the influence of school, family and area of residence on the incidence of youth unemployment. We summarise below the results of three studies carried out between 1945 and 1960.

The first, and most influential, study was by Ferguson and Cunnison.[14] They carried out a survey of 1349 fourteen-year-old boys who left school in Glasgow in January 1947. It was a period of strong demand for labour; juvenile unemployment averaged only 1.6 per cent, and 85 per cent of the boys went straight from school to their first jobs.

Four-fifths of the school-leavers had definite careers in mind. Most were looking for skilled manual work, although in many cases their teachers regarded such aspirations as unrealistic. The most common reason for choosing a job was the interest of the work; parents' wishes were not a major factor, even less the boy's desire for status and income. At the end of three years most boys were still in occupations for which they had expressed a preference when leaving school, although many of the boys who had expressed no preference were by then in unskilled work.

A number of influences on occupational choice were isolated (Table 2.5). Entry into skilled manual work was inversely related to the size of family, the quality of the residential area, and the quality of home life (as assessed by social workers). The influence of the father's occupation,

TABLE 2.5   Distribution of occupational status according to potential influences on occupational choice

	Percentage distribution by status				
Influences	*Skilled manual*	*Semi-skilled manual*	*Unskilled manual*	*Non-manual*	*Total*
Father's occupation					
Skilled manual	51·6	9·2	13·1	26·1	100·0
Semi-skilled manual	49·4	10·9	14·9	24·8	100·0
Unskilled manual	44·7	11·2	22·6	21·5	100·0
Non-manual	47·2	12·1	12·7	28·0	100·0
Family assessment					
Good	50·9	9·9	15·4	23·7	100·0
Fair or bad	34·2	14·5	25·2	26·1	100·0
No. of children in family					
1–4	50·1	12·0	12·8	25·1	100·0
5 +	42·9	10·2	22·9	24·1	100·0
Position of boy in family					
1st or 2nd child	47·7	11·7	16·8	23·8	100·0
5th and over	41·3	8·5	23·0	27·2	100·0
Residential area					
Good or fair	52·3	8·7	13·2	25·8	100·0
Slum	31·1	12·6	27·4	28·9	100·0
Accommodation					
Less than 2 per room	51·9	12·2	14·4	21·5	100·0
4 or more per room	37·1	12·6	24·6	25·7	100·0
Family structure					
Unbroken	48·2	10·9	16·3	24·6	100·0
Broken	39·4	11·8	24·8	24·0	100·0

Source: T. Ferguson and J. Cunnison, *The Young Wage-earner: A Study of Glasgow Boys* (London: Oxford University Press, 1951), Table 35. Reproduced by permission of The Nuffield Foundation.

although discernible, was surprisingly small. It had no impact on
school-leavers' preferences, although there was a tendency for sons of
skilled workers to have greater success in achieving skilled status,
perhaps because of the inability of low-paid workers to afford
apprenticeships for their sons.

Frequent job-changing was characteristic of the young workers. On
average they changed jobs once a year, although there were considerable differences between them. Nearly one quarter of the boys remained
with the same employer throughout the three years, while 14 per cent
changed employers five times or more. Frequency of job change was
inversely related to job status, size of family, quality of residential area,

quality of home life and regular attendance at school. Job-changing was particularly common among younger children in large families, and where the father was unskilled or his employment record was poor.

The reasons for changing jobs varied according to the frequency of job-changing (Table 2.6). Those who changed only once tended to change in order to begin an apprenticeship, to obtain promotion or to improve long-term prospects, while those who changed more often tended to do so for higher wages, because of dissatisfaction, or because they were dismissed for absenteeism or misdemeanours.

TABLE 2.6   Distribution of predominant reasons for changing job, according to number of jobs held

No. of jobs	No. of boys	Predominant reason for change (%)					
		Voluntary leaving				Dis-missal	Total
		Apprentice-ship, pro-motion, and prospects	Wages	Dis-like of job	Other reasons		
1–2	483	71·2	8·7	5·8	9·5	4·8	100·0
3–4	123	29·2	16·3	38·2	11·3	5·0	100·0
5 +	61	10·0	11·4	44·2	26·2	8·2	100·0
All groups	667	57·9	10·3	15·3	11·4	5·1	100·0

Source: Ferguson and Cunnison, *op. cit.*, Table 30.

At the end of three years, 74 per cent of the boys considered that they had obtained the kind of work they wished to remain in permanently. Over 96 per cent of skilled workers were permanently settled, as were 63 per cent of the semi-skilled; but 64 per cent of the unskilled considered their latest job to be merely a 'stop-gap' until something better was found. Over 80 per cent of those who were settled had chosen the job themselves. Half of these said they had chosen it for its interest, while one-third of the remainder had chosen it for its security. Wages were a less important factor, and indeed their wages were on average lower than the wages of those who were in stop-gap employment, though only marginally so. Fewer of those in stop-gap employment had chosen the job themselves, and, where they had, wages were relatively more important to them and the interest of the jobs much less so. Ferguson and Cunnison suggest that the differences between those in settled and those in stop-gap employments reflect underlying differences between young workers in their attitudes to work. If the attributes of the two categories of workers are compared, it is found that those in stop-gap employments change jobs more often, have a greater tendency to experience unemployment when job-changing, are more hostile to work, less well trained, and more prone to dismissal.

It is clear that there are many economic and social influences on youth unemployment and that these are related in a complex way. Some of the most important concern the young workers' personality and family background; their net effects are summarised in Table 2.7. However, not all aspects of family background operate as might be expected. For example, Ferguson and Cunnison found that the families of working widows tend to have very satisfactory employment records, while 'only children' lose a relatively large proportion of working days on grounds of sickness. Observations such as these suggest that the degree of responsibility experienced by the young worker at home may be a more important influence on his employment record than the standard of living provided for him. It is clearly dangerous to draw general conclusions about social influences on youth unemployment without very detailed evidence.

A survey by Harris of 3960 school-leavers in 1954–5 provides evidence on the relationship between educational background and job-changing.[15] The study distinguished between grammar and technical schools on the one hand – which cater for higher-ability children who leave school late – and secondary-modern and all-age schools on the other hand – which tend to cater for low-ability children who leave school early.

Of those leaving grammar and technical schools, on average 67 per cent of boys and 58 per cent of girls did not change jobs in the first two years. 12 per cent of boys and 13 per cent of girls changed more than once, but only 3 per cent of boys and girls changed more than twice. Of those leaving secondary-modern and all-age schools, somewhat fewer did not change jobs at all, i.e. 49 per cent of boys and 44 per cent of girls. Twice as many boys and girls changed jobs more than once and about four times as many – 13 per cent of boys and 11 per cent of girls – changed jobs more than twice. These results indicate that, while on average the propensity to change jobs is greater among secondary-modern school-leavers, the difference is almost entirely accounted for by the existence of a hard core of persistent job-changers among those leavers.

Harris's study also suggests that there is considerable social mobility

Youth Unemployment

TABLE 2.7   Incidence of unemployment according to family background and
boy's personal characteristics

Influences on unemployment	Amount of unemployment in three years (%)			
	None	Less than 3 months	3 Months or more	Total
No. of children in family				
1–2	73·5	18·7	7·8	100·0
3–4	70·1	22·1	7·8	100·0
5–7	64·6	26·5	8·9	100·0
8 +	57·2	30·7	12·1	100·0
Position of boy in family				
1st or 2nd	69·9	21·0	9·0	100·0
3rd or 4th	67·3	26·7	6·0	100·0
5th or later	55·7	31·2	13·1	100·0
Scholastic assessment at age 14				
A or B	71·8	21·3	6·9	100·0
C	69·0	22·5	8·5	100·0
D	64·9	26·1	9·0	100·0
E	54·7	32·2	13·1	100·0
Personality assessment at age 14				
A	72·4	19·0	8·6	100·0
B	67·8	24·1	8·1	100·0
C	58·8	29·0	12·2	100·0
Mother's status				
Working out of home	71·2	19·0	9·8	100·0
Not working out of home	67·3	25·3	7·4	100·0
Dead	51·5	25·8	22·7	100·0
All boys	66·7	24·4	8·9	100·0

Source: Ferguson and Cunnison, *op. cit.*, Tables 89–93.

in the labour market. Although there is a positive association between the father's occupation and that of his children, the association is a fairly weak one, and is largely unaffected by the job-changing behaviour of the young workers.

Carter studied a sample of 200 fifteen-year-olds – 100 boys and 100 girls – who left five secondary-modern schools in Sheffield in 1959.[16] Although not primarily concerned with youth unemployment, Carter's work provides interesting corroborative detail on earlier studies.

Although it was a time of full employment, the young people interviewed by Carter appeared to take a realistic – if not cynical – view of their prospects. This attitude seemed to reflect an awareness of their own limitations, rather than an informed view of employment opportunities. Few had very strong preferences for one kind of work as compared with another, although there appeared to be an agreed hierarchy of occupations: for boys apprenticeships conferred most social standing, while for girls office work, shop work and factory work were ranked in that order.

Most had jobs arranged when they left school, and few found any difficulty in obtaining work. However, much job-searching was carried out hurriedly in the last fortnight before leaving school, and often the first job offered was accepted.

Very few jobs were obtained through official channels; both workers and employers regarded the Youth Employment Service as dealing in second-class jobs for second-class people. Many good jobs, such as apprenticeships, were arranged through family contacts, while a surprisingly large number (17 per cent of first jobs) were obtained simply by calling on the employer 'on the off chance'.

Perhaps because of the chance nature of job placement, the association between IQ and the skill level of the first job obtained, although positive, was not very high. However, the association strengthened over time, because of the relatively high drop-out rate among apprentices with low IQs.

Thirty-six per cent of boys and girls changed jobs within the first year. Change of occupation – rather than just change of employer – was more common among boys than among girls. Eleven per cent of boys and 8 per cent of girls had at least three jobs. Most quit their jobs because of dissatisfaction, either with the nature of the work or with the prospects for promotion. Dissatisfaction with apprenticeships was fairly common, even among those who continued in them. None of the young people found trade unions of any assistance to them: at the end of the year only 15 per cent of boys and 11 per cent of girls were members of trade unions, and in each case the initial contact with the union was concerned exclusively with recruitment. Had the young people had more contact with either the management, the union or the Youth Employment Service, it is possible that some of their problems could have been resolved on the spot; as it was, grievances tended to build up until the worker was prompted to quit.

2.6 RECENT STUDIES

Since the early 1960s there has been a discernible trend for unemployment to increase proportionately more among young workers than among other age groups. It appears to be a general phenomenon among developed countries, although it has been particularly noticeable in the United States. There is a widespread belief that the explanation lies in voluntary job-changing by young workers who find it increasingly difficult to settle into working life. This has focused research on the job-changing habits of young people.

Baxter carried out two surveys of youths in Sheffield, covering those born in 1952 and 1956 respectively.[17] The first survey was confined to chronic job-changers, i.e. those who changed jobs on average more than twice a year for the first three years of their working life. 115 chronic job-changers were identified; each was followed from school-leaving age (fifteen) up to twenty, and some up to twenty-two. Although job-changing dropped sharply at eighteen and again at nineteen, it remained fairly stable thereafter at a rate well above the average for all young people. The second survey covered 7000 school-leavers and followed each for a three-year period.

The studies reveal that young people as a whole are particularly prone to dismissal for disciplinary reasons, especially absenteeism and bad timekeeping; in this respect the experience of chronic job-changers does not differ significantly from the norm. The probable explanation is that young workers find it difficult to adapt to the discipline of working life.

A relatively high proportion of chronic job-changers are employed in distribution, where dismissal for disciplinary reasons seems to be particularly common. Baxter suggests that the large number of small firms and the relative weakness of union representation may explain the high rate of dismissal in distribution. It is well known that the quit rate is also high in distribution. Baxter's results suggest that dissatisfaction with hours and conditions is the main reason for the relatively high quit rate. It appears that among young workers dissatisfaction with pay, promotion and training is no greater than in other trades, while dislike of the job is much less common in distribution than other trades. Although Baxter's results need to be interpreted with care, they suggest that the frequency of job-changing among young people owes something to the primitive personnel policies of small firms, who use hiring and firing *in lieu* of a more sophisticated system of screening applicants.

In 1973 a nationwide survey of 1479 registered unemployed was carried out by Daniel, and three years later a follow-up study was made of their subsequent careers.[18] Although not primarily concerned with the young unemployed, one of the main findings was that fewer young people thought it important to find a job than did the unemployed in the prime age group. Daniel's explanation is that young people have fewer financial responsibilities, and so experience less hardship when they are unemployed.

The startling increase in unemployment since the onset of the world recession in 1973 has further underlined the importance of research into youth unemployment. Official agencies in a number of countries have commissioned studies of youth unemployment, and at the moment there is a great deal of work in progress.

In the UK the Manpower Services Commission recently sponsored several surveys concerned with youth unemployment.[19] The two most important are the Young People Survey, a national random sample of 3074 sixteen- to nineteen-year-olds, and the Employers Survey, based on interviews with the senior personnel officers of 701 establishments in the private sector, the nationalised industries and local government. Both surveys were carried out in November 1976.

The Employers Survey reveals the disadvantages that unqualified young people suffer from when seeking employment. Table 2.8 lists the criteria used for screening job applicants, shows their relative importance for different types of work, and indicates the employers' rating of young people relative to other applicants according to each criterion. On the whole young people show up badly, particularly on literacy, numeracy, attitude to work, appearance and ability to communicate. Indeed, the only factors in their favour derive from their superior physique and fitness. Other factors – specific educational qualifications and willingness to join a union – are of less importance generally, and are associated with only a marginally higher rating for young people.

On average employers believe that the calibre of young applicants is declining, and most of those who think it is improving attribute this to the increasing supply of young people, which allows them to 'cream off' more easily. Given a choice between recruiting young people and alternatives such as upgrading existing employees, recruiting from other firms and hiring housewives returning to work, most employers indicate a clear preference for one of the alternatives. This suggests that in the long term the increasing labour-force participation of housewives poses a serious threat to the employment prospects of less well-qualified young people.

The Young People Survey indicates that attitudes to work have not changed a great deal since prewar days. Most young people in

TABLE 2.8   Employers' view of essential and desirable characteristics of job applicants: a comparison of young people with other recruits

	Percentage stating attribute essential to all recruits	*Net rating of young people relative to older recruits*[a]
Willingness/positive attitude to work	76	−32
Basic '3 Rs'	50	−34
Good level of numeracy	39	−34
Good level of general physical fitness	39	+18
Presentable appearance/tidiness	38	−28
Good written English/literate	36	−42
Ability to communicate well verbally	30	−25
Mature/stable	24	−50
Specific educational qualifications	23	+5
Specific physical attributes	21	+16
Willingness to join union	15	+5
Past experience	10	−57
Existing union membership	5	−7

Source: Manpower Services Commission, *Young People and Work: Research Studies* (London: HMSO, 1978), Table 7.2. Reproduced by permission of the Controller of HMSO.

[a] Calculated by substracting the percentage of respondents who thought young people were worse on each attribute from the percentage thinking they were better.

employment appear satisfied˙ with their jobs, and most consider satisfaction to be the single most important aspect of a job; the unemployed place much less emphasis on job satisfaction and far more emphasis on good wages. As secondary factors, those in employment attach more importance to friendly atmosphere and promotion opportunities than do the unemployed.

Informal methods of job search still predominate, with official agencies having a relatively small role to play: 31 per cent of first jobs were found through personal contacts or family influence, 15 per cent by direct approach to the employer, and another 15 per cent by replying to newspaper advertisements; in 4 per cent of cases the employer had approached the school. Only 28 per cent of first jobs were found through Careers Offices or Employment Exchanges.

2.7 SUMMARY AND EVALUATION OF EARLIER STUDIES

Before summarising the results of the surveys, it is appropriate to examine some of their more important limitations.

The principal shortcomings stem from the sampling methods employed. There are three main methods of sampling the young unemployed: using surveys of households, records of school-leavers, and registers of the unemployed.

In principle a household survey can provide a fully representative sample; in practice its main disadvantage is cost. This has meant that in the past household surveys have been confined to urban areas, where the concentration of population is high; relatively little has been discovered about youth unemployment in rural areas, or in rural industries such as agriculture and forestry. There is also the question of whether young workers in residential hostels should be included; these workers may have special characteristics which make it misleading to consolidate them with the rest of the sample.

A sample based on school-leavers has the disadvantage that it excludes those going on to further education, as well as new immigrants, and so on. It therefore needs to be supplemented by other surveys, but in practice this has not usually been done.

A sample of the registered unemployed is biased against those who have little incentive to register, such as those who are not entitled to unemployment benefit, or who regard their chances of finding a job through official agencies as negligible.

Another limitation – applicable to some surveys much more than to others – is the small size of the sample, and the consequently wide confidence intervals which are associated with the statistical estimates. The problem is not severe for the major features of unemployment, which have been repeatedly studied and on which a definite picture has emerged. But it does affect some of the inferences drawn from special aspects of the situation, which may have been considered in just one or two studies and concern only a small proportion of the population of young people.

The ideal study would be based on a nationwide household survey, covering such a large proportion of households that the statistical accuracy of sample estimates would be guaranteed. This is not a utopian proposition: the results reported in Chapter 5 relate to just such a sample.

Subject to the qualifications noted above, youth-unemployment studies suggest that throughout the twentieth century there have been a number of 'constants' in the situation, which are summarised below.

(1) There are significant differences between the employment ex-
    periences of skilled and those of unskilled workers. Young unskilled
    workers tend to enter 'blind-alley' occupations in which career
    prospects are poor; only a small proportion of workers continue in
    these occupations as adults. The unskilled change jobs very
    frequently, moving in an apparently haphazard way, often mot-
    ivated only by dissatisfaction with their present work. Skilled
    workers, on the other hand, pursue long-term career development,
    changing jobs much less frequently – and then often to broaden
    their experience within their chosen trade.
(2) Employers of young unskilled workers take little interest in their
    welfare. They appear to be intolerant of their difficulties in adjusting
    from school to work. The social gulf between young and old makes
    dismissal for disciplinary reasons and quitting without notice all too
    common. In most trades relying on young people it is cheaper to
    hire and fire casually than to screen job applicants carefully and to
    follow grievance procedures before separation. An employer can
    tolerate high wastage of labour if he can rely on a ready supply of
    new recruits from the next generation of school-leavers. So long as
    each new generation is happy to enter these trades, employers will
    have little incentive to improve their personnel policies.
(3) Trade unions have done little to promote the interests of young
    workers. It is far easier for an employer to dismiss a young worker
    than an older worker. Craft unions do not normally oppose the
    laying-off of apprentices when their training is complete, and have
    done little to improve their pay relative to other workers'. Perhaps
    older workers recognise that the low wages paid to apprentices help
    to subsidise the higher wages paid to craftsmen; so long as increased
    recruitment of apprentices does not threaten existing jobs, it may be
    in the older workers' interests to acquiesce in the use of cheap
    apprentice labour.
(4) Job placements of young people are organised very informally: in
    particular, surprisingly little use is made of official agencies. The
    young worker's family is valuable in providing an information
    network about prospective vacancies, in arranging introductions,
    and even in bringing influence to bear on employers.
(5) A large proportion of unemployment among young workers is
    accounted for by a relatively small number of 'chronic job-
    changers'. These typically come from unsatisfactory homes, where

others are prone to unemployment, and live in poorer areas. On the other hand, the chronic job-changers are also a small proportion of the young workers with deprived backgrounds: in each generation a large number of young workers from poor families obtain better jobs than those of their parents.

Finally, it must be recognised that long-term unemployment among school-leavers has been a transitory phenomenon, typically emerging in the later phases of a recession and disappearing as soon as an upturn begins. It is of course quite possible that it will emerge as a characteristic of post-energy crisis society. But the pattern of youth unemployment so far – which has been a relatively stable one – lends little support to this view. It may be that topical interest in the problems of unemployed school-leavers has directed attention away from the more profound problems of the youth labour market noted above.

3 Modern Theories of Unemployment

3.1 INTRODUCTION

The 1970s have witnessed a revival of interest in the theory of unemployment. The prewar dogmas of the classical economists and the early postwar dogmas of the Keynesian school have been swept away. In their place is a growing body of literature which analyses unemployment by examining its microeconomic foundations.[1]

It is the object of this chapter to present the theory of unemployment as it appears in the light of recent analytical developments. The discussion is, however, at a very elementary level, and only those aspects of the theory directly relevant to this study are considered.

Section 3.2 introduces the basic concepts of labour-market theory. Section 3.3 enumerates the various imperfections in the labour market and discusses their implications. Sections 3.3–3.9 consider in turn the major categories of unemployment, while sections 3.10 and 3.11 analyse the incidence of unemployment in different groups of workers. The applications of the theory to youth unemployment are developed in Chapter 4.

3.2 THE FUNCTION OF THE LABOUR MARKET

The function of the labour market is to match people to jobs. Not all people are equally suitable for a given job, nor are all jobs equally suitable for a given person. So far as the suitability of a person for a job is concerned, there are certain individual characteristics which must be taken as fixed – notably age, sex and ability – and some which can, at some cost, be changed – notably the individual's skills and place of residence. So far as the suitability of a job for an individual is concerned, there are certain aspects of the job specification which are difficult to change, such as the type of work to be done and the industry in which it is to be carried on. Other aspects are more easily changed, notably the skill required of the worker and the location of the job. We may therefore visualise the labour market as matching a labour force characterised by age, sex and ability to jobs characterised by occupation and industry, the matching being effected through training and through the relocation of industry and labour.

A labour market is efficient if it satisfies two main criteria. The first is that of *allocative efficiency*, which means that each worker should be employed in the occupation to which he is most suited, in terms of his occupational preferences and his comparative advantage with respect to other workers. The second is that of *full employment*, which means that each worker willing to work at the wage currently paid to individuals of similar skills can find suitable employment. It is well known that both types of efficiency are achieved by a competitive market economy operating under ideal conditions.[2]

Allocative efficiency is achieved by a system of wage differentials. Given a structure of differentials, the market allows employees to reveal their preferences for one occupation over another, and employers to reveal their preferences for different types of skill. If when aggregrated by the market the plans of employers and employees are inconsistent, the wage differentials are adjusted by competitive forces until they become consistent. With the resulting system of differentials no worker is willing to exchange occupations and no employer wishes to substitute skills.

Full employment is achieved by adjustment of the general level of real wages. At a given real wage there are a certain number of individuals seeking work and a certain number of employers offering vacancies. If the number of jobs sought exceeds the number of vacancies available, there is an excess supply of labour. Competition to fill the vacancies leads workers to bid wages down. This normally discourages people from entering the workforce, while it persuades employers to increase their demand for labour at the expense of other factors of production. Thus demand increases, supply contracts, and the excess supply of labour is eliminated.[3]

3.3 IMPERFECTIONS IN THE LABOUR MARKET

In practice no economy ever satisfies the idealised conditions of a competitive market economy. Imperfections in the labour market inhibit adjustment to full-employment equilibrium. While the economy may have a long-run tendency to full employment, the conditions which determine the level of full employment are continually changing, so that the system is always in pursuit of a moving target; thus, at any point in time the economy is some distance from equilibrium.

There are six major imperfections which are potential causes of unemployment.

(1) *Money wages may be rigid downwards.* In this case an excess supply of labour cannot be eliminated by a reduction of money wages. But workers may be willing to work for a lower real wage brought about by a rise in prices. This is the case of 'involuntary' or 'Keynesian' unemployment.[4]

(2) *Transactors may have limited knowledge.* Workers may have little information about wages and conditions in alternative occupations, and employers may lack knowledge of workers' abilities. Workers therefore prefer to 'shop around' for jobs when unemployed, rather than take the first job offered; likewise, employers may be reluctant to fill a vacancy with the first applicant. This type of unemployment is known as 'search unemployment'. Search unemployment and unfilled vacancies can coexist for as long as it takes to match up the unemployed job-seekers to the vacancies available.

(3) *The loss of income owing to unemployment may be artificially reduced*, either by subsidies from relatives or by unemployment benefit. This reduces the incentive to find new employment quickly, and encourages the enjoyment of unemployment as a form of leisure.

(4) *Wage differentials may be fixed by institutional considerations, and may be out of line with competitive differentials.* This can create unemployment in 'overpaid' categories of labour. The unemployed have an option of transferring to underpaid work (for which there is excess demand), or remaining unemployed on the chance of getting an overpaid job when a vacancy arises. The term 'queue unemployment' has been used to describe the status of those who choose to wait for a vacancy in overpaid work.

(5) *The provision of certain types of training may be hampered by the lack of transferable property rights in trained labour.* Underprovision of training reduces the occupational choice of unemployed workers and may lead to 'structural unemployment'. Similar effects may be produced by institutional obstacles to the geographical mobility of labour.

(6) *Changing jobs may be costly*, so that workers in seasonal and casual

trades prefer to remain unemployed during slack periods rather than change jobs to fill in their time.

3.4 INVOLUNTARY UNEMPLOYMENT

Keynes argued that workers stipulate a minimum money wage, rather than bargain directly for a real wage, so that at a certain level the money wage is rigid downwards. In Figure 3.1 the equilibrium real wage, W_0, is determined by the intersection of the demand and supply of labour schedules; at this equilibrium wage there is full employment of N_0. Suppose now that the real wage is initially at a higher level, W_1. If the money wage is rigid downward, the labour market cannot adjust to equilibrium by a reduction of the money wage. Transactions must therefore take place at the disequilibrium wage W_1. Since contracts in the labour market are voluntary, the amount of labour actually employed will be equal to the minimum of the amount demanded and the amount supplied. Hence N_1 workers are employed and $N_2 - N_1$ are unemployed.

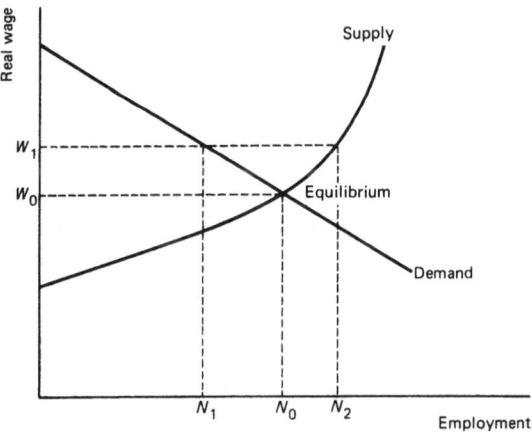

FIGURE 3.1   Disequilibrium in the labour market

Note that, when there is unemployment, those fortunate enough to be employed receive a higher real wage than they would at full employment (W_1 compared to W_0). Although this may seem surprising, it is in fact borne out by statistical evidence: for example, at the time Keynes was writing, during the Great Depression, the standard of living of those in employment was relatively high. The unemployed are willing to work for a lower real wage than that prevailing, but because money wages are rigid downwards the lower real wage cannot be brought about by a fall in money wages. Only if the real wage is reduced through higher prices can the unemployed be set to work.

Now, it is clear from Figure 3.1 that, at the prevailing real wage W_1, workers plan to supply labour at a rate N_2 and therefore anticipate an income of $W_1 L_2$. At the same time employers plan to produce an output sufficient to meet workers' expenditure of $W_1 N_1$. Thus, at least initially, a shortage of output to the value of $W_1 (N_2 - N_1)$ may be anticipated. In an idealised market economy this would drive up money prices and thereby reduce the real wage to its equilibrium value. But in practice this does not happen. Workers may be unwilling to commit themselves to expenditure before their employment has been finalised, and, even if they were willing, the absence of forward commodity markets would make it difficult for them to communicate their consumption plans to entrepreneurs.[5] Since prices will not rise spontaneously, Keynesians argue that the only way to achieve full employment is to stimulate the demand for labour artificially – for example, by public spending or a cheap-money policy.

Keynes suggested two reasons for money-wage rigidity. The first is workers' money illusion. Workers are not conscious of changes in money prices, and are therefore unwilling to accept wage cuts when prices fall, although they will tolerate constant money wages when prices rise. However, this argument needs to be modified for the postwar period, in which most workers have become inflation-conscious. It could be argued instead that workers systematically overestimate the rate of inflation, because in any bundle of commodities they notice price rises more than they notice price reductions. If workers bargain to maintain a real wage, price inflation will have to fall substantially before workers will accept any reduction in the customary increase in the money wage.

The second reason is that workers regard the main function of money-wage bargaining to be the preservation or enhancement of wage differentials *vis-à-vis* other groups of workers. Because the dates of annual wage settlements for different groups of workers are staggered throughout the year, any group of workers agreeing to a reduction of money wages will – at least temporarily – also suffer a reduction in wage relative to other groups.

As they stand, the arguments above are incomplete, because they assume that workers in employment are in a position to insist on a negotiated minimum money wage. However, in the long run workers in employment can prevent wage cuts only if they are immune from competition from the unemployed. If the unemployed offer to work for less than the prevailing money wage, employers could in principle sack existing workers and take on new ones. In practice, immunity from competition can arise in a number of ways.

Firstly the unemployed may act altruistically and refuse to compete, out of loyalty to fellow workers. In small communities with strong social ties this may be an important factor. Secondly, the unemployed may find it demeaning to compete, or may be concerned that they will be working alongside others who are paid more for the same job. Thirdly, the unemployed may be optimistic about their chances of finding employment without bidding down the money wage; this is quite probable in a boom, but most unlikely in a prolonged recession. Fourthly, employees may be able to use their strike-threat power to prevent employers recruiting cheaper labour. However, this power depends critically on the employers' inability to replace the entire workforce. If the strike is begun at short notice, the employer's only chance is to obtain replacements from the pool of unemployed. If the pool is large enough, and contains men of sufficient skill, then the strike threat may be nullified. In most industries, though, these conditions are not satisfied. Moreover, the employees can always increase the size of the replacement workforce required by arranging sympathetic action by the employees of suppliers or contractors.

Finally, it has recently been suggested that money-wage rigidity may be a consequence of workers' ignorance of the prevailing wage rate in the labour market as a whole.[6] Suppose that each worker knows only of the wage rate paid by his own employer. He is happy to continue working at the negotiated wage until, as a consequence of falling product prices, his employer confronts him with a choice between taking a cut in wages or being made redundant. Being unaware of the general fall in prices and the fact that labour is now a buyer's market, he believes he can obtain employment elsewhere at his existing wage, and therefore accepts redundancy in order to search for a new job. Only after searching for some time does he recognise his mistake, and become willing to accept employment at a lower wage. By this time prices may have fallen even further, so that his expectations must be revised downward again before he is re-employed.

It can, of course, be argued that, if money wages are not naturally flexible downwards, then cuts in money wages should be enforced through statutory powers. Keynes believed that such a policy would be self-defeating. A moderate reduction in money wages, engineered by the government at the onset of a recession, would have an adverse effect on entrepreneurs' expectations. The anticipation of a further fall in money wages would encourage entrepreneurs to postpone their investment, and thereby reduce the demand for labour. Only if the fall in money wages were so drastic as to create an expectation of a future rise in money wages would the effect be reflationary. However, changes of this magnitude in money wages would so reduce the liquidity of money that it would cease to function as a medium of exchange, and wages would become fixed in terms of some other commodity instead.[7]

3.5 SEARCH UNEMPLOYMENT

The theory of search unemployment emphasises (a) that the choice of a suitable job requires a great deal of information if alternative employments are to be properly appraised, (b) that information in the labour market is usually incomplete, so that searching for information about jobs is a valuable activity, and (c) that search activity is often better carried on full-time rather than part-time.[8]

Two types of information are relevant to job choice: namely, the nature of the job – the effort involved, the skills required, and so on – and the remuneration – the rate of wages, promotion prospects, occupational pension, and so forth. In a perfectly competitive labour market it can be assumed that all employers in the same area will offer the same remuneration for the same job. But in practice lack of information among workers may encourage some employers to discriminate against the uninformed by offering low wages to those unaware of alternative job opportunities.[9] In such cases there are gains to searching not only across occupations but also across employers, in order to obtain the most favourable wage quotation.

The appropriate strategy of job search depends on the type of information sought. Consider first the search for information on wages. For most manual or low-paid jobs the wage is usually announced when the vacancy is notified; in order to search for information it is sufficient to scan classified newspaper advertisements, visit employment exchanges, or just telephone around. For professional or highly paid jobs the wage is normally negotiated, usually after the applicant has been interviewed; in this case wage-search is a more time-consuming process.

Obtaining information on the nature of jobs is usually more difficult than obtaining wage quotations. The worker can search *extensively*, by collecting summary information on a large number of jobs, using advertised job specifications, brochures, and so on, or *intensively*, sampling a few jobs in depth – for example, by working at them for a probationary period. The strategy adopted will depend on the strength of the job-seeker's preferences for a particular type of work, and on how much he already knows about alternative occupations. Normally, extensive search will precede intensive search. Extensive search can usually be carried on part-time, while intensive search is typically a full-time occupation.

Job search may be initiated for a number of reasons.

Firstly, all new entrants to the labour force are job-seekers: school-leavers, graduates, immigrants, discharged servicemen, ex-prisoners, and so on, all come into this category. There is an increasing tendency for people to enter and leave the labour force several times: mature adults taking full-time education, and housewives returning to work after child-bearing are two examples of this.

Secondly, the individual's life-cycle may lead him to prefer different sorts of jobs at different ages. The young worker looks for sociable work near to his parents' home, the prime-age worker with dependents looks for well-paid work (even though working conditions may be un-pleasant), while the older worker looks for lighter jobs. Thus there are certain points of transition in working life where the worker starts to look around for a different sort of employment. This applies parti-cularly to manual work, where the state of health of the worker is important, and to unskilled work, where training requirements do not impede entry into a new occupation.

Thirdly, structural changes in the economy may call for a re-distribution of the working population. Some industries expand, while others contract; industries in one region prosper, while industries in other regions decline; and changes in technology alter the relative demands for different skills. These changes are reflected in job losses in one place and newly-created vacancies somewhere else. Job search will continue for as long as it takes redundant workers, or those who have quit because of worsening wage differentials, to match themselves to suitable vacancies in the growth areas.

Finally, there are other, less systematic, factors which induce job search. Possibly the most important are dissatisfaction with a job which has failed to realise expectations, and dismissal by the employer for disciplinary reasons.

The impact of job-search unemployment depends on the proportion of the working week devoted to search. If search is a full-time activity, the worker will be wholly unemployed; while, if it is part-time, the worker will at most be underemployed, i.e. work fewer hours per week than he otherwise would: he may arrange absence from work, forego overtime, or dispense with a secondary occupation. In some cases, part-time job search may be entirely at the expense of leisure.

The number of people unemployed through full-time job search depends on both the frequency and duration of job search. The frequency, denoted f, is measured by the average number of times per year the worker changes jobs, while the duration, d, is measured by the average time (in years) elapsing between leaving one job and starting the next. Each year the average time spent unemployed, u, is equal to the product of frequency and duration.

$$u = f \times d$$

Given a homogeneous stationary working population, u determines the percentage unemployment rate of the population as a whole.[10]

In practice there is, of course, considerable variation in both frequency and duration of unemployment of different workers at the same time, and also in the working population as a whole at different times. Some of the reasons for individual differences have already been considered: they reflect personal differences in job preferences, access to information, and the ability to derive satisfaction from work. However, other factors are especially important where the duration of unemployment is concerned.

The gains from full-time job search arise from the expected increase in welfare associated with finding a better job (or getting a job if one has been made redundant). The costs of full-time job search arise from the psychological costs of being subjected to screening by employers, the direct costs of search not refunded by potential employers, and the current income foregone in not taking 'fall-back' employment (if it is available).

Suppose that the job-seeker can estimate the probability that out of any given number of applications he will be offered a job yielding more than some specified reward. Then he can compute the optimal number of jobs to sample before he terminates search: the optimal duration of search is set at the margin where the expected increase in the reward from the best available job offered is equal to the cost of an additional job application. In general, the greater the anticipated dispersion of rewards, the longer will be the duration of search.[11]

In some cases the expectations of the job-seeker will be mistaken. As his search proceeds it will become evident that his estimates of the probability of success will have to be modified. Given the natural optimism of job-seekers, this modification usually involves a downward revision of expectations. This process adds to the duration of search, since in the early stages of search the worker's excessive ambition leads him to apply for jobs for which competition is intense, and to reject worthwhile job offers as too low. Thus, workers who are overoptimistic, and reluctant to revise their expectations, will tend to have a longer duration of search.[12]

3.6 BENEFIT-INDUCED UNEMPLOYMENT

Benefit-induced unemployment describes the classic response of 'rational economic man' to unemployment benefit (or, indeed, to any state or private benefits for which loss of earnings makes him eligible). The response is to prolong the duration of unemployment – whether for leisure or job search – and thereby reduce the time spent at work.[13]

Suppose that an individual works a standard forty-hour week, but can increase his leisure by taking seasonal or casual weekly work, or by taking spells of unemployment between regular jobs. If there is no unemployment benefit, the trade-off over the year between income and leisure is described by the line AB in Figure 3.2. If there is a weekly unemployment-related benefit equivalent to an annual sum OC then his trade-off is modified to the line AD. The individual's preferences for income as against leisure are represented by a family of indifference curves. Each indifference curve represents the combinations of income and leisure which provide a given level of satisfaction. Two indifference curves are shown in the diagram: each is convex to the origin, illustrating that, as income is reduced, more and more leisure is required to compensate for a further loss of income: in other words, an increment of income is valued less the more income one has already.

The rational worker chooses the most preferred income–leisure combination, which diagrammatically is shown by the point of tangency between the indifference curve and the trade-off locus. Following the introduction of unemployment benefit, the worker moves from the point E, with an income of X_1 and leisure of Y_1, to the point F, with an income of X_2 and leisure of Y_2.

It can be shown that unemployment benefit has two distinct and

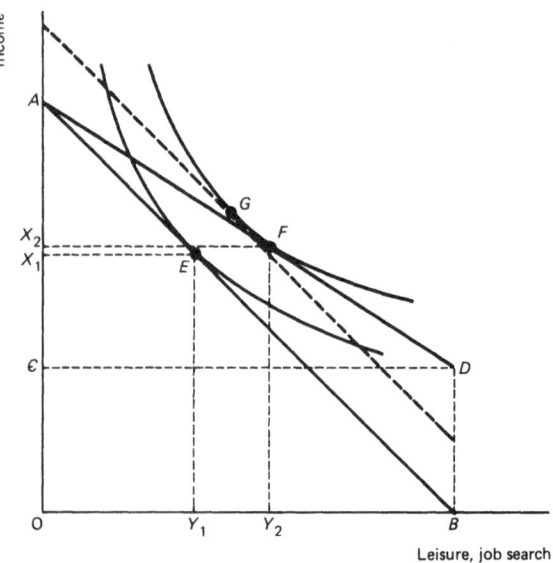

FIGURE 3.2   Effect of benefits on unemployment

reinforcing effects on worker behaviour. Firstly the potential welfare of
the worker is increased (even if the relative income derived from work
and unemployment remain the same). Being better off, he will normally
consume more of each of the 'goods', in this case income and leisure.
The additional consumption of leisure is shown in the diagram by the
movement from the point *E* to the point *G*. Secondly, the change of the
relative rewards to work and leisure induces a substitution of leisure for
work; this is shown by the movement from *G* to *F*. It can be seen that
these two effects normally reinforce one another in increasing the
amount of leisure, which in the present context means increasing the
amount of unemployment.

  In certain cases unemployment benefit may improve the allocative
efficiency of the labour market. If workers have no means of financing
consumption during periods of unemployment – i.e. they have no
savings and are unable to borrow against prospective future income –
then they may be forced to take the first job that becomes available,
even though it may be better to wait until they can find a more suitable
job. Unemployment benefit allows them to continue searching and –
provided it does not discourage them from accepting a suitable job

when it is offered – improves the allocation of labour. In this case unemployment benefit takes the place of a loan, which cannot be provided because of imperfections in the capital market. In so far as the 'loan' element in the benefit improves placements, it may reduce future separations and so actually diminish the amount of unemployment.

It must also be recognised that the graphical analysis makes a number of simplifying assumptions which have the effect of understating the costs of leisure. To begin with, the worker who takes occasional employment has to search more frequently for work than does a worker who is regularly employed. Since search does not give the same benefits as leisure, nor afford the same income as employment, it clearly constitutes a deterrent to intermittent employment. Further, all governments impose certain restrictions on the payment of unemployment benefit: it is not paid immediately to people who quit, and those who unjustifiably refuse work may be temporarily disqualified. Unless an individual can somehow evade these screening procedures (which are specifically designed to minimise benefit-induced unemployment), the returns to unemployment may be relatively small. Finally, benefit-induced unemployment has been disputed on the grounds that many people are habituated to work, and have a strong desire for regular employment. For these people work confers status and satisfies a need for independence and financial security. However, if there are any people in a position to indulge in periodic unemployment without great risk, and with a positive preference of leisure and variety in working life, they are probably young people. On these grounds the analysis warrants serious consideration in any study of youth unemployment.

3.7 QUEUE UNEMPLOYMENT

Queue unemployment is an example of unemployment created by social and institutional constraints on the labour market. For various reasons wage differentials in different occupations may not reflect the relative scarcities of labour in those occupations. Some occupations will therefore have an excess supply of potential entrants.

Suppose these occupations recruit at random when a vacancy occurs – for example, by taking the first person who calls inquiring about a job. If the chances of obtaining a job are fairly good, then a full-time job-seeker calling regularly on high-wage employers may have a higher present value of expected future earnings than a worker with a secure low-wage employment. The pool of full-time job-seekers in high-wage occupations will expand until the chances of obtaining a job are reduced to a level which equates the expected values of the two income streams.[14] Thus, so long as equivalent occupations pay different wages, there will be a pool of unemployed job-seekers waiting for entry into the higher-wage occupations.

3.8 THE TRAINING PROBLEM AND STRUCTURAL UNEMPLOYMENT

The theory of structural unemployment is based on a disaggregated view of the labour market. The market is regarded as a collection of sub-markets for different levels and types of skill.[15]

The theory assumes that different skills have low elasticities of substitution in both demand and supply. In other words, it is difficult for an employer to substitute one skill for another in carrying out a particular job, and it is equally difficult for a worker trained in one skill to adapt readily to another.

In a changing economic environment, where some industries are growing and others are in decline, it is difficult to maintain each labour sub-market in equilibrium. With free markets wage differentials would adjust, encouraging employers to take on the more abundant types of labour, and workers to switch into occupations where demand is greatest. But in practice two factors usually prevent this. The first is institutional fixing of wage differentials, considered in the previous section. The second is the inadequate provision of training, which inhibits the transfer of workers between occupations.

There are good grounds for arguing that there is underprovision of training in the private sector.[16] The absence of transferable property rights in trained labour means that workers cannot easily mortgage their future income to finance their own training. In practice the prospective employer may be willing to finance it, provided that he can 'lock in' the trainee until he has repaid the costs of his training out of increased productivity. There are various ways of locking in employees: offering pensions which are forfeited on quitting, giving low-interest mortgages which have to be repaid, and so on. However, none of these methods offers the employer full security, and to the extent that the risk of quits cannot be eliminated the employer will be reluctant to invest in training.

Just as institutional constraints restrict the mobility of workers between occupations, so they also restrict mobility between locations.[17]

Many industries are tied to particular areas, because of reliance on local raw materials and specialised transport networks. For this reason changes in industrial structure often lead to regional imbalances in growth. The readjustment of the working population through migration is inhibited by the natural reluctance of workers to break social ties. But, in addition to this, institutional factors deter movement. Nationally negotiated wage rates prevent regional wage differentials from reflecting the relative scarcities of labour. The need to wait for council housing and the loss of continuity in children's schooling both create problems in moving. Thus, even if the underprovision of training could be resolved, there would still be problems of structural adjustment arising from obstacles to the geographical mobility of labour.

3.9 SEASONAL AND CASUAL UNEMPLOYMENT

Seasonal unemployment refers to unemployment in trades affected by an annual cycle – for example, agriculture and tourism.[18]

In principle it is possible for a worker in seasonal trades to hold a 'portfolio' of jobs which keeps him fully employed throughout the year – for instance, ice-cream salesman in the summer, ski-instructor in the winter. On balance, though, there are probably more seasonal jobs available in the summer than in the winter. Nevertheless, if workers in summer jobs were really anxious to work in the winter, they could bid down winter rates in certain industries in order to secure employment. Suitable industries would be those making intensive use of non-union labour to produce easily stored goods (for instance, the toy industry). However, there are good reasons why seasonal workers may prefer to enjoy full-time leisure for part of the year: it avoids the psychological cost of repeatedly adjusting from one type of work to another, it may be possible to draw unemployment benefit to finance leisure activities, and, even if no benefit is forthcoming, the opportunity for prolonged leisure may be the basic reason for choosing seasonal employment in the first place. It can therefore be argued that at least some seasonal unemployment is voluntary, and represents a deliberate withdrawal from the labour force to enjoy full-time leisure.

Casual unemployment occurs in trades affected by employment fluctuations of high frequency and large amplitude.[19] The difference between these and seasonal trades – apart from the obvious one that the cycles may not be annual – is the unpredictability of the fluctuations. The typical casual trade has occasional and unforeseen demands for large teams of workers to work for short periods – an example is dock work. Because the work has to be begun at short notice, it is necessary to have a pool of unemployed workers held in readiness for work.

Recent years have seen a growing tendency for the decasualisation of trades. In some cases this has been a direct consequence of mechanisation or improved production planning. In other cases there has been no change in production methods; only the contractual relationship between employer and employee has changed. The employer has assumed the role of an insurer of wage income, replacing a randomly fluctuating income stream with a constant income stream of equivalent value. This movement has been encouraged by governments because it makes it easier to tax wage payments. Although the insurance of wage-income has probably been of mutual benefit, the long-term labour contract has reduced the flexibility of the labour force by requiring employees to be in readiness for work at times when it is highly improbable that their services will be required. As such, decasualisation may simply conceal unemployment.

3.10   IMPLICATIONS FOR THE INCIDENCE OF UNEMPLOYMENT

Each of the preceding theories has implications for the incidence of unemployment in different groups. At any one time the following groups will be much more strongly represented among the unemployed than they are among the working population as a whole.

(1) *Workers who overestimate the general level of wages and prices prevailing in the economy.* Such workers are likely to stipulate too high a money wage, and will therefore be unable to obtain suitable offers of employment.

(2) *Workers who are reluctant to adjust their expectations in the light of search experience.* Such workers will tend to continue longer in unemployment before they can find a job which meets their expectations; hence their duration of unemployment will be long.

(3) *Workers with little knowledge of the nature of alternative jobs, or those undecided on a career.* Such workers will search intensively for jobs, sampling each for a probationary period until they find one which suits them. Their frequency of job-changing will be high.

(4) *Workers who are subsidised (by either their family or the state) while unemployed.* Their loss of earnings owing to unemployment is

relatively low, and this encourages them to remain unemployed longer than they otherwise would.

(5) *Wealthy workers who can maintain consumption standards while unemployed.* By dissaving – for example, by liquidating assets such as building-society deposits – workers can finance themselves through a period of unemployment, and avoid being forced to take the first available job to satisfy immediate consumption needs.

(6) *Workers seeking employment in trades where wages are artificially high.* When wages are above the competitive level, workers are encouraged to wait rather than accept a job in a low-wage occupation.

(7) *Workers who wish to enter trades in which there is underprovision of training and who are not sufficiently adaptable to take alternative work.* Given that institutional arrangements prevent these workers from bidding down wages, they may become structurally unemployed.

(8) *Workers in seasonal and casual trades,* who either enjoy the opportunities for leisure or experience high costs of alternating jobs.

3.11 DISCRIMINATION

Discrimination is another factor which influences the incidence of unemployment in different groups. It can occur in either recruitment or redundancy.

When recruiting workers, employers have incomplete knowledge about the various qualities of job applicants. The costs of obtaining detailed information about each applicant can be very high, particularly when it has to be checked with third parties. Employers may therefore choose to screen applicants on the basis of clearly visible characteristics, which they believe are associated with the qualities for which they are looking.[20] This does not necessarily imply a particular view about cause and effect: only a belief in a statistical association between the frequency with which the characteristic is observed and the frequency with which the particular quality is present. For this reason, employers may discriminate against

– workers with poor educational attainments, who are unlikely to be either intelligent or industrious;
– workers who have been absent through sickness in the past, and who

are likely to lose more days through sickness in the future;
- workers with bad physique, or judged to be of poor appearance, who are unlikely to be suitable for strenuous work, or for representing the employer in his dealings with the public;
- workers from particular ethnic groups, residents of particular areas, or people in particular age groups, who are believed to have generally poor employment records.

Discrimination in redundancy involves a number of relatively complex issues.

In any organisation the informal understandings built up between colleagues serve to reduce administrative costs. Since it takes time for these understandings to be built up, the newest recruits are likely to be least well integrated into the organisation. The loss in overall team performance is likely to be minimised when it is the newest recruits which are made redundant – i.e. when a last-in first-out (LIFO) redundancy policy is implemented. This tendency is likely to be strengthened where unions are able to influence redundancy policy, since the longest-serving members are most likely to dictate local union policy.

The liability of employers for redundancy payments may also encourage a LIFO policy, since payments are normally related to length of service, so that it is cheaper to dismiss the most recent recruits. On the other hand, it must be recognised that redundancy may provide a welcome opportunity to shed less efficient workers, so it is by no means in the interests of employers to stick rigidly to a LIFO policy.

In skilled trades, under certain conditions, there may be discrimination in redundancy between trainees and qualified workers. In the extreme case where all workers, whatever their level of training, are remunerated in direct proportion to their current productivity, there is no incentive to implement redundancies selectively according to the level of training. This is the case where all employees wholly finance their training costs out of current income. However, when training is very costly, such a method of financing may not be feasible, and the firm itself steps in as an investor. In this case the firm's redundancy policy is no longer neutral with respect to trainees and fully trained labour. By making redundant a new trainee rather than an older worker the firm is able to postpone its investment in the uncompleted part of the training, although at the expense of having to repeat the completed part of the training programme later when the qualified worker retires and his replacement is hired. An analysis of this situation from the point of view of a profit-maximising employer suggests that the optimal redundancy policy is to dismiss either the most recently recruited trainees or the qualified workers nearest to retiring age. The group least vulnerable to redundancy consists of workers who have just completed their training. However, this conclusion may need to be modified in trades where, for institutional reasons, qualified workers are entitled to excessively high rates of pay.

4 Theories of Youth Unemployment

4.1 INTRODUCTION

This chapter presents a number of hypotheses about youth unemployment, derived from the analysis given in the previous chapter.[1] The hypotheses have been grouped according to the particular aspect of youth unemployment with which they are concerned. Sections 4.2–4.7 explain why a relatively high level of youth unemployment persists even during periods of prosperity. Sections 4.8 and 4.9 are concerned with the cyclical sensitivity of youth unemployment, while section 4.10 considers various explanations of the rising postwar trend.

Each section concludes with predictions derived from the hypotheses. In Chapter 6 these predictions are tested using evidence from the EEC Labour Force Sample Survey, and from earlier studies of youth unemployment.

4.2 JOB-SEARCH HYPOTHESIS

This hypothesis is concerned with the job-search strategy of less able young workers. It is based on two propositions: (1) less able workers tend to leave school as early as possible, and so for the first few years of their working life are economically dependent on their family; and (2) because of their recent entry into the working population they are unfamiliar with the work environment, and because of their youth and low ability they have problems in adjusting to it.[2]

(1) A dependant's contribution to family finances is normally fixed on his ability to pay, so that the proportion of marginal wage income which the dependant retains for his personal discretionary use will be small. When he is earning a low wage the family will provide his basic needs free of charge, while if he is earning a good wage he may

have to pay the full cost of board and lodging. It follows that, when choosing a job, the net gain to the dependant from taking a higher-paid job will be much less than the wage differential. For a self-interested dependant, a rational criterion of job selection will place relatively great weight on the non-income attributes of a job, since these do not have to be 'shared' with the rest of the family. Such attributes include the quality of the working environment, the quality of social life among the employees, the convenience of travel to work, and so on. Thus, job search will be directed to discovering the non-income attributes of jobs, rather than to evaluating the wage differentials between them.

(2) The fact that young people have only recently entered the working population means that they have relatively little prior knowledge of the non-income attributes of jobs. The type of information they require will therefore be difficult to obtain through advertisements, and may not be too easy to find through employment exchanges either. Personal contact with existing employees provides a more relevant type of information, but most useful of all is the experience provided by a probationary period of employment. The disadvantage of this last method of search is that, until the required type of employment is found, the frequency of job-changing will tend to be high and hence the proportion of working life spent unemployed will also tend to be high. However, the fact that the young worker is taking each job partly for experience means that he need not be too selective, so that his average duration of unemployment between jobs will tend to be short.

This analysis does not extend to more able young workers, for a variety of reasons: (a) more able young workers tend to leave school later than their less able counterparts, and consequently are less likely to be dependants for long; (b) because of their greater ability, they are more likely to think in terms of career development and will therefore place greater weight on long-term income prospects when choosing a job; and (c) more able workers are likely to undergo on-the-job training and will therefore be less mobile between firms. Workers undergoing training will change jobs relatively infrequently because of the benefits of maintaining continuity in their training. Workers may remain immobile after training if they are 'locked in' by pension schemes and the like as part of the firm's strategy to recoup its investment in training.

The theory therefore predicts that the high rate of unemployment among young people is associated with a high frequency of job-changing by the less able workers. Since the job-changing is voluntary, a relatively high proportion of job losses among young people will be accounted for by resignation rather than dismissal. The major reason for job search among young people will be dissatisfaction with their present employment. Finally, young people will tend to use informal methods of job search, such as personal contact, rather than more formal methods, such as visiting employment exchanges.

4.3 SEASONAL-UNEMPLOYMENT HYPOTHESIS

This hypothesis is based on the proposition that young people place a much higher value on leisure than do adults. We have already argued that, because they are subsidised by their families, young people tend to undervalue wage income. But there is a more general proposition, that, irrespective of the subsidies they receive, young people manifest an unusually strong preference for leisure. Possible reasons are that they become accustomed at school to short working days and relatively long holidays, and that they find the disciplined environment of school and work rather irksome, and appreciate the autonomy which leisure affords.

There are three ways of indulging a preference for leisure: choosing a job with a short working week and long holidays, taking regular spells of unemployment between jobs, and obtaining jobs of a seasonal or casual nature. From the employee's point of view, a regular employment with a short working week and long holidays would probably be most suitable, but for a variety of reasons – mainly concerned with the 'overhead' costs of employment – few employers are willing to offer these terms. Those employers that do – for instance, schools and universities – do not normally offer jobs suitable for young people (because of the qualifications that are required). Young people are therefore obliged to take their leisure by other means.

Seasonal and casual employments offer two main advantages over interrupted regular employment. Firstly, because the work is expected to be temporary, the loss of a job does not prejudice the opportunity of working again for the same employer; thus seasonal and casual employments may be a safer option in the long run. Secondly, employers who recognise the potential for recruiting young people may find it profitable to adapt the job specification to young people's needs: for example, seasonal jobs in tourism often allow work to be combined with outdoor leisure pursuits.

On the other hand, a policy of interrupted regular employment allows a wider range of jobs to be taken. If, as has been suggested, job-changing represents the pursuit of variety in work, then seasonal or casual work which remains the same from year to year may prove unattractive.[3]

Subject to this qualification, the theory predicts that a relatively high proportion of young people will enter seasonal and casual trades, and that the rate of unemployment among young people will be closely connected with the numbers in these trades. There will be a seasonal pattern in youth unemployment which will resemble the fluctuations in activity in the seasonal trades. More generally it suggests that redundancies among young people in seasonal and casual trades are analogous to quits in other trades, in so far as the redundancies each year are foreseen by the employee, and could be avoided, if desired, by choosing an alternative occupation.

4.4   STRUCTURAL-UNEMPLOYMENT HYPOTHESIS

Structural unemployment caused by the difficulties of retraining redundant skilled workers does not seem relevant to youth unemployment, because, by and large, young people constitute the least skilled but most adaptable section of the labour force. However, it is to be expected that regional immobility of labour will be a factor in youth unemployment, just as it is in unemployment generally. But it is difficult to see how it can explain the relatively high incidence of unemployment among young people. It is true that teenagers are strongly attached to their families and are therefore, in this sense, immobile. But the same reasoning suggests that teenagers will move wherever the family moves; they move together with the family rather than away from it. Thus, the geographical mobility of teenagers will be more or less the same as that of older workers who have teenage children. On the other hand, young adults – particularly those just married – are in a good position to move away from their families, and it is well known that this age group is particularly mobile. It appears, therefore, that, while structural unemployment may well be an element in the youth-unemployment problem, it cannot be this element which accounts for the severity of unemployment among young people.

4.5 LIFE-CYCLE HYPOTHESIS

The life-cycle hypothesis asserts that the employment of young people is likely to be concentrated in certain industries where wages are low and long-term career prospects are poor. This provides a direct incentive for young people sooner or later to change jobs, in order to move out of these trades. But, since training also tends to be poor, their chance of obtaining skilled employment elsewhere is low; after quitting their job they are likely to find skilled jobs closed to them, and they must therefore remain unemployed until they reconcile themselves to unskilled work.

It has already been suggested (section 4.2) that young people place relatively great weight on the non-income attributes of jobs. Two non-income criteria are particularly germane to our argument: that the work environment should be a social one, with plenty of opportunity for establishing personal relationships, and that the work should be fairly close to home, so that the out-of-work environment may be stabilised while acclimatisation to work is accomplished.

Employers who can offer jobs with these attributes will be able to fill them at relatively low wages, provided they are happy to rely heavily on young workers. Employers who recognise the importance of juvenile labour may make special efforts to recruit direct from school, and emphasise to young workers the social advantages of working with colleagues of the same age as themselves. Furthermore, some employers may take advantage of the fact that young workers are not income-conscious, and therefore do not search very hard for high wages. They may make a point of offering very low wages which only badly informed young workers will accept. On each of these grounds, young people's emphasis on the non-income attributes of jobs is liable to lead them into low-wage occupations.

The concentration of young people in low-wage occupations has two main implications.

The first is the inevitability that sooner or later most of them will have to leave to find other work. As they become older, get married, leave home and acquire financial responsibilities, they become more conscious of the low income associated with their job, and therefore leave to seek better-paid work.

Secondly, because the turnover of young workers is high, substantial expenditure on training will not be worthwhile for the employers. This applies particularly to those who exploit the lack of wage information among young workers, for as soon as the workers discover they are underpaid they will quit. Although general business education is not the main purpose of on-the-job training, most such training contains at least some element of it. Workers deprived of on-the-job training are therefore unlikely to have developed any aptitude for skilled work. Thus, when they leave to seek better-paid jobs they have little chance of finding skilled employment. They must obtain high wages by either doing unskilled work in uncongenial surroundings, or joining a union which has substantial bargaining power.

There are of course other reasons why young people are concentrated in certain industries. They are normally ineligible for jobs of a very responsible or hazardous nature, jobs with long hours or extensive shift-working, and jobs which rely on graduate recruitment. Entry is difficult into trades dominated by the self-employed, where considerable capital and good market contacts are necessary to conduct a successful business. In some cases employers may discriminate in favour of young people because of their fitness and agility. But, while these considerations are undoubtedly significant in influencing the age composition of certain industries, their overall effect is unlikely to call for a substantial modification of the preceding argument.[4]

The predictions of the theory are that young workers will be concentrated in low-wage industries which offer no training and no long-term career prospects. Labour turnover will be highest where the wages are lowest. The highest rates of unemployment will occur when workers attempt to switch out of these industries in their late 'teens or early twenties. Most workers leaving these industries will take higher-paid unskilled jobs of a less congenial kind.

4.6 QUEUE-UNEMPLOYMENT HYPOTHESIS

This hypothesis is based on the proposition that in certain trades institutional factors determine age-related wage differentials which fail to reflect the competitive position of different age groups in the labour market. It is argued that in these trades adult labour is relatively overpriced, so that young workers coming of age are made redundant. But the high adult wage encourages them to wait around for the chance of obtaining a higher-paid job in the same industry.

In trades employing unskilled labour there may be a statutory minimum wage for adult labour which is above the competitive level. Since the work is unskilled there may be little difference in the productivity of youths and adult workers. If the minimum youth wage is only a fraction of the adult wage, the institutional wage differential will overstate the competitive differential between the two groups of workers.

In skilled trades the system of age-related wage differentials may be the outcome of collective bargaining between craft unions and employers' associations. A primary objective of union negotiators is to protect the interests of adult workers. Such a policy can be justified on the grounds of the family responsibilities of the typical adult worker, although in practice it may simply reflect the influence of older workers in the union hierarchy. Union bargaining power may be used to raise the adult wage but not the youth wage. So long as the union has the power to control the number of youths employed, the adult wage can be raised indefinitely relative to the youth wage. This does not threaten the job security of existing adult workers so long as the average wage paid by the employer allows him to make a normal profit. In fact, it may be in the interests of adult workers to have a large number of youths employed, as the employer's profit from youth labour may be used to subsidise an increase in the adult wage.

A consequence of the overpricing of adult labour is that the number of youths employed may be far greater than the number of higher-paid vacancies available for them when they come of age. The worker who has entered the industry as a youth, and cannot obtain immediate employment as an adult, has a choice of remaining unemployed in order to wait for a high-paid vacancy, or taking a lower-paid job in another industry. In some cases there may be limited opportunities for self-employment, but this appears to be the exception rather than the rule. Normally a proportion of young adults will remain unemployed, forming a 'queue' for any vacancies that arise.

Thus, the theory predicts that youth unemployment will be associated with redundancies among young workers who have reached an age where they are eligible for higher-paid work. The redundancies will be concentrated in unskilled trades where wages are normally at the statutory minimum, and in skilled trades where the differential between the apprentice's wage and the craftsman's wage is relatively high.

4.7 BENEFIT-INDUCED UNEMPLOYMENT HYPOTHESIS

The state benefits for which unemployed young workers qualify tend to be much lower than those paid to adult workers. (This applies both to unemployment benefit itself, and to earnings-related benefits for which the unemployed qualify through loss of income.) However, because young workers receive relatively low wages, the benefits, though small in absolute terms, may be significant in relation to the loss of earnings due to unemployment. But more important is the fact that state benefits constitute only a small proportion of the total benefits received by young people.

As mentioned earlier, young people – particularly those living with their parents – are normally subsidised by their families to a considerable extent. This has two direct effects on unemployment. First, it reduces the young worker's net loss of earnings during unemployment and encourages him to spend a larger proportion of his time either enjoying leisure or searching for a job. Secondly, it eliminates the need for income to satisfy immediate consumption needs; given that most young workers have very small savings to draw on, they might otherwise be forced to take the first job they could find that pays an adequate wage.

This suggests that youth unemployment, like unemployment generally, will be highest in countries where state unemployment and earnings-related benefits are most generous. It also predicts that unemployment will be highest among young workers who are dependants (i.e. live with their families) and among those from wealthy families, where other members earn sufficient to provide a high level of subsidy.

4.8   SCHOOL-LEAVER HYPOTHESIS

This section and the next are concerned with possible explanations of the cyclical sensitivity of youth unemployment.

It is an obvious point that all new entrants into the working population have to find a job, while those already established in the workforce normally have a job they can remain in if they wish. But it does not follow from this that new entrants are necessarily prone to unemployment. Entry into working life can usually be planned, and a first job arranged so that there is no intervening period of unemployment.

Nevertheless, it can be argued that during a recession one particular category of new entrants – namely, school-leavers – is prone to unemployment. The basis of the argument is that school-leavers have little flexibility in adjusting to poor employment prospects in the labour market.

The population at any one time may be divided into three groups: the employed and the unemployed (who together constitute the working population), and non-participants. There is constant circulation from group to group. In particular, there is movement into unemployment both from among the employed – owing to redundancy, or workers quitting to search for better jobs – and from among non-participants – owing to young people's leaving school or college, housewives' returning to work after raising a family, and so on.

In a recession the number of unfilled vacancies contracts and the number of unemployed rises. Thus the probability that anyone seeking a job will be able to find one within a given time is reduced; openings are scarce, and there is a large stock of people waiting to apply for them. This will influence the flow into unemployment from the different groups.

In the early stages of a recession, firms may cut back their workforce very quickly, faster than the natural rate of decrease through retirement. Workers made redundant will swell the ranks of the unemployed. But, as the pace of recession slackens, further reductions may be fully accommodated by retirements. In that case, the only employees becoming unemployed will be those who voluntarily quit. But few people will quit if the probability of obtaining a new job is small: they prefer their existing job, however unsatisfactory, when it is a choice between that and no job at all.[5]

Throughout the recession there will be a steady stream of non-participants planning to enter employment. These people will be hoping to enter vacancies created by either (a) an increase in total demand for labour, (b) retirements or voluntary withdrawals, and (c) quits. But there are no new jobs being created, retired workers are not being replaced, and very few people are quitting. Thus potential entrants have a choice of either entering the workforce to become unemployed, or deferring their entry until the chances of employment improve.

For some groups postponement of entry may be quite acceptable. For example, housewives may be willing to continue looking after their families, or may devote themselves to voluntary work. But for school-leavers there is usually only one alternative – continued education – although in some cases military service may be an option. Continued education is unlikely to prove attractive to less able young workers, and a high proportion are therefore liable to become unemployed. For those who do continue, education affords only a short-term postponement of entry into working life. If the recession is a long one, continued education can have little effect in reducing the supply of young workers.

We have argued that, of the various groups of workers who become unemployed, redundant workers are a transitory phenomenon at the onset of a recession, quitting workers and housewives re-entering the working population respond quickly to the worsening employment situation, while school-leavers respond relatively little. Thus, when the recession has set in, the proportion of school-leavers among the newly unemployed will rise, and before long school-leavers will predominate among the total unemployed.

The situation would not be so serious if it were the more able young workers who were most at risk in the labour market, for in the long run they might benefit from continued education. But, as we shall argue below, it is the least able young workers who are most susceptible to unemployment – the very workers for whom continued education, at least in its present form, is likely to be of least benefit.

When there is an excess supply of labour, each advertised vacancy will have a large number of applicants. The employer will be able to 'cream off' by insisting on high qualifications; in some cases he may insist on unnecessary qualifications simply to reduce the selection problem to manageable proportions. Thus workers who would normally qualify for a particular job may no longer do so in a recession. They may just qualify for a lower-status job for which they would normally be overqualified. At each level those who normally enter there face competition from more highly qualified applicants, and are forced out into lower-level employment. In other words there is an 'occupational ladder', and during a recession everyone steps down one or two rungs.[6] Naturally those forced out at the bottom are the least well-qualified applicants, who would normally take unskilled jobs. Thus, in a recession the burden of unemployment falls most heavily on those whose educational attainments are lowest. Almost by definition, they are the people least likely to benefit from continued education.

The predictions of the theory are that youth unemployment is likely to be very sensitive to fluctuations in the state of employment generally. In a recession the young will constitute an unusually high proportion of the unemployed, and of the young unemployed a high proportion will be first-job seekers; a large proportion of the young unemployed will have low educational attainments. Among the unemployed as a whole the number of quits will fall sharply, as will the labour-force participation of married women. But continuation of education will increase only marginally.

4.9   SELECTIVE-REDUNDANCY HYPOTHESIS

In the previous section the role of redundancies was played down, and it was suggested that they are likely to be significant only at the onset of a recession. However, it can be argued that redundancies contribute to youth unemployment, because employers discriminate against young people when selecting candidates for redundancy.

Firstly, when employers finance on-the-job training, the profit-maximising redundancy policy is to dismiss the newest trainees and the qualified workers nearest to retiring age. Since the profit-maximising training policy is normally to recruit very young trainees, redundancy among new trainees will fall most heavily on young people.

Secondly, employers may follow a LIFO policy, either to retain the key members of the organisation, or as part of an informal agreement to reward length of service with job security, or as an indirect way of promoting the interests of older workers. LIFO is likely to discriminate against the young both because of their recent entry into working life and because their frequent job-changing reduces their average period of employment.

Thirdly, when there are redundancy payments which increase with length of service, employers will, for obvious reasons, tend to discriminate against the young.

These arguments suggest that the incidence of redundancy may be relatively high amongst the young. Thus, in the early stages of a recession, when redundancies are likely to increase sharply, young workers will constitute an unusually high proportion of the newly unemployed. By the time redundancies begin to fall, young workers may constitute a significant proportion of the total unemployed.

4.10   TREND HYPOTHESES

Theories concerning the increasing trend in youth unemployment are necessarily controversial, since most of them invoke alleged changes in social attitudes and in social structure, which are, in principle, difficult to measure. Two main approaches are considered here.

The first argues that the frequency of job-changing is increasing because of mounting dissatisfaction with the type of work available in industrial economies, and because of increased social tolerance of unemployment.

Methods of production are at an intermediate stage between craftsmanship and complete automation. Division of labour has developed a large number of highly specialised routine jobs, but computerisation has not yet succeeded in fully mechanising them. Dissatisfaction with the job encourages employees to quit in order to find more interesting work, but the scarcity of such work means that they may have to sample several jobs before settling down. It has been argued that, in the postwar period, education has encouraged unrealistic job aspirations among young people, so that they experience more dissatisfaction than older workers. Older people also tend to be more conservative in their job-changing habits, and prefer to demonstrate their frustration through strikes and other disruptive action. Dissatisfaction therefore shows up most clearly in the increasing frequency of job-changing among young people.

In the postwar 'welfare state', unemployment has lost much of its social stigma. Once again, the new attitude is most likely to be expressed in the behaviour of young workers. Increasing tolerance of unemployment reduces inhibitions about quitting jobs, or risking dismissal for absenteeism or bad work. As such, it will reinforce the tendency toward increasing frequency of job-changing among young workers.

The second approach analyses the trend in youth unemployment in terms of changes in the demand and supply of youth labour. It is argued that as a result of these changes the equilibrium real wage for youth labour has fallen relative to that for other groups. Given that there is some rigidity in wage adjustments, this has led to an increasing excess supply of youth labour.

There is reason to believe that in the postwar period the supply of youth labour has increased while the demand has fallen. Supply has increased mainly for demographic reasons – that is, owing to the early postwar increase in the birth rate. Demand has fallen, because the increasing labour-force participation of housewives has established an alternative source of low-wage labour. From the employer's point of view this source has a number of attractions: workers tend to be more mature, and therefore present fewer disciplinary problems, many have had previous work experience (prior to raising a family) and they are believed by most employers to be better educated (i.e. more literate and numerate).

A fall in demand, coupled with an increase in supply, implies a reduction in the equilibrium real wage. But, if the real wage cannot be reduced – for example, because of minimum-wage legislation, or because of a lack of wage information in the market – an excess supply of labour will emerge. This will show up in terms of an increased duration of unemployment among young people. It is likely that the rate of unemployment will be highest in industries where the female labour force has increased most significantly.

5 Statistical Evidence for West Germany, Italy and the UK, 1973 and 1975

5.1 INTRODUCTION

This chapter reviews the statistical evidence on youth unemployment provided by the EEC Labour Force Sample Surveys of 1973 and 1975. Although the surveys cover all member countries, this study examines only three countries: West Germany, Italy and the UK. The criteria governing the selection of these countries are discussed in Chapter 1.

The Labour Force Sample Survey covers approximately one in 200 of all households in each country; its scope and limitations are described in detail elsewhere.[1] The results of the survey are broadly consistent with the official statistics of the countries concerned. Where differences emerge, the EEC data are generally to be preferred. This is because most official statistics rely on surveys of the registered unemployed, which are liable to omit those who have no incentive to register but are actively seeking a job. Where official statistics are based on household surveys the sample is usually much smaller than for the EEC survey, and so the confidence regions for the statistics tend to be larger. In fact the EEC sample is so large that in most cases the effect of purely random sampling error is likely to be negligible.[2] Any exceptions to this are noted in the text.

However, when interpreting the statistics certain qualifications should be borne in mind, particularly when making comparisons across countries.

Although the surveys were synchronised in the sense that they all took place in the spring, they were carried out over different periods in the different countries and were typically spread over several weeks. In view of the seasonality of school-leaving, and also the rapidly changing economic climate during 1975, unemployment rates – particularly among teenagers – may not be strictly comparable.

The survey results are based on respondents' own descriptions of their situation. Questions had to be translated into different languages, and, although strenuous efforts were made to ensure that the correct idiom was used in each country, there may well be differences in respondents' interpretations of some of the questions. Furthermore, respondents' descriptions of their circumstances are conditioned by the economic and social climate, which varied considerably from country to country.

This chapter restricts itself to comments on the main features of the survey data. The interpretation of the evidence, in relation to theories of youth unemployment, is considered in Chapter 6.

5.2 DURATION OF SEARCH

Table 5.1 presents evidence on the duration of search of unemployed workers in selected age groups. For each age group the table shows a frequency distribution of the time for which individuals were seeking jobs prior to the date of the survey. It should be noted that this is not the same as a frequency distribution of the time it takes to find a job. In a cross-section study of a population of job-seekers, the two distributions will be the same only when the probability that an individual will find a job is independent of the time for which he has already been searching.[3] Typically, in a cross-section of job-seekers, the probability of finding a job diminishes as the time already spent searching increases. In this case it is known that the average time spent searching prior to the date of the survey exceeds the average time required to find a job. The reason is that the stock of job-seekers at any one time necessarily contains relatively few of the individuals who are quickly placed and a relatively large number of the individuals who experience difficulty in finding a job.

The evidence is that in West Germany and the UK the duration of search among young men is significantly lower than average. In West Germany this is particularly true of teenagers: in 1973 85 per cent of teenage job-seekers had been searching for less than six months, compared with 71 per cent of job-seekers as a whole. In the UK about 65 per cent of both teenagers and young adults had searched for less than six months, compared with 47 per cent for job-seekers as a whole. In Italy the average duration of search is exceptionally high, and there is little difference between young people and the working population as a whole in the average duration of search. In 1975 the differences between teenagers and others tend to be smaller, although the underlying pattern is much the same.

TABLE 5.1 DURATION OF SEARCH Percentage distribution of duration of search, for selected age groups, 1973 and 1975

(a) West Germany: men

Duration of search (months)	Age group						
	14–15	16–19	14–19	20–24	25–29	30–34	All ages
1973							
less than 1	–	33·6	30·9	35·0	32·7	26·4	27·6
1–2	24·4	20·3	20·6	20·4	35·1	28·3	22·8
3–5	50·0	31·9	33·3	15·2	23·6	22·8	20·1
6–11	25·6	10·3	11·6	18·1	8·6	6·8	13·8
12 +	–	3·9	3·6	11·3	–	16·7	15·8
Total	100·0	100·0	100·0	100·0	100·0	100·0	100·0
1975							
less than 1	15·0	13.6	13·7	17·0	14·4	9·9	10·4
1–2	32·6	26·3	26·7	31·9	30·5	25·9	25·4
3–5	28·6	25·9	26·1	24·8	25·3	29·8	28·2
6–11	23·8	22·6	22·7	19·1	21·0	24·7	23·4
12 +	–	11·6	10·8	7·2	8·8	9·7	12·5
Total	100·0	100·0	100·0	100·0	100·0	100·0	100·0

(b) Italy: men

Duration of search (months)	Age group						
	14–15	16–19	14–19	20–24	25–29	30–34	All ages
1973							
less than 1	6·9	2·7	3·6	5·8	3·8	5·8	6·0
1–2	16·5	10·0	11·4	6·1	7·4	12·3	8·7
3–5	21·2	14·9	16·2	19·6	16·5	22·3	20·1
6–11	40·9	30·8	32·9	32·5	21·1	21·7	28·8
12 +	14·5	41·6	35·9	36·0	51·2	37·9	36·4
Total	100·0	100·0	100·0	100·0	100·0	100·0	100·0
1975							
less than 1	11·1	4·8	5·8	4·8	3·5	7·0	6·7
1–2	13·7	8·2	9·0	8·1	8·6	8·0	9·0
3–5	32·4	19·4	21·4	17·4	18·8	15·2	20·5
6–11	18·7	35·8	33·2	31·4	26·9	43·3	30·5
12 +	24·1	31·8	30·6	38·3	42·2	26·5	33·3
Total	100·0	100·0	100·0	100·0	100·0	100·0	100·0

(c) UK: men

Duration of search (months)	Age group				
	14–19[a]	20–24	25–29	30–34	All ages
1973					
less than 1	29·8	26·7	20·3	16·5	17·2
1–2	21·7	21·2	20·8	14·7	14·7
3–5	12·5	18·7	18·0	15·9	15·5
6–11	19·0	15·9	18·0	14·2	16·2
12 +	16·9	17·5	22·9	38·7	36·3
Total	100·0	100·0	100·0	100·0	100·0
1975					
less than 1	28·7	25·5	23·8	17·0	20·3
1–2	32·0	34·4	27·8	25·7	25·6
3–5	17·6	15·1	17·6	16·7	16·7
6–11	15·6	15·2	16·6	21·5	18·0
12 +	6·1	9·8	14·2	19·1	19·3
Total	100·0	100·0	100·0	100·0	100·0

[a] In the UK there are no under-sixteen-year-olds eligible for full-time employment.

(d) West Germany: women

Duration of search (months)	Age group						
	14–15	16–19	14–19	20–24	25–29	30–34	All ages
1973							
less than 1	39·8	28·7	29·8	43·0	27·2	39·7	25·8
1–2	20·4	44·6	42·2	30·1	31·2	26·6	35·9
3–5	39·8	20·8	22·6	20·0	22·3	16·6	19·3
6–11	–	3·9	3·6	2·2	14·0	10·6	8·9
12 +	–	2·0	1·8	4·7	5·3	6·5	10·1
Total	100·0	100·0	100·0	100·0	100·0	100·0	100·0
1975							
less than 1	7·7	11·5	11·1	18·1	14·2	14·3	12·8
1–2	47·9	31·2	32·7	26·0	28·6	18·9	24·6
3–5	20·1	24·8	24·4	28·3	26·7	34·4	27·1
6–11	24·3	24·7	24·8	18·7	28·6	22·6	24·7
12 +	–	7·8	7·0	8·9	3·9	9·8	10·7
Total	100·0	100·0	100·0	100·0	100·0	100·0	100·0

(e) Italy: women

Duration of search (months)	Age group						
	14–15	*16–19*	*14–19*	*20–24*	*25–29*	*30–34*	*All ages*
1973							
less than 1	5·7	2·8	3·2	2·4	4·8	9·6	4·6
1–2	15·8	6·4	7·9	2·1	7·4	7·5	5·9
3–5	13·7	18·9	18·1	11·4	17·3	22·2	19·1
6–11	52·8	39·6	41·7	33·2	24·4	33·9	33·0
12 +	12·0	32·3	29·1	50·9	46·1	26·8	37·4
Total	100·0	100·0	100·0	100·0	100·0	100·0	100·0
1975							
less than 1	23·6	4·5	7·4	5·1	7·7	7·8	7·3
1–2	8·7	5·4	6·3	4·7	7·0	3·3	6·0
3–5	14·8	20·5	19·5	12·0	12·1	13·8	16·2
6–11	48·6	47·1	37·6	24·0	23·5	36·0	36·1
12 +	4·3	22·5	19·4	40·7	49·2	51·6	34·5
Total	100·0	100·0	100·0	100·0	100·0	100·0	100·0

(f) UK: women

Duration of search (months)	Age group				
	14–19	*20–24*	*25–29*	*30–34*	*All ages*
1973					
less than 1	38·5	34·7	36·4	25·4	30·8
1–2	23·7	27·9	19·3	18·2	21·6
3–5	13·6	16·0	16·3	25·2	17·4
6–11	15·7	7·8	19·5	18·3	14·3
12 +	8·5	13·6	8·4	12·9	15·9
Total	100·0	100·0	100·0	100·0	100·0
1975					
less than 1	35·4	37·8	34·6	29·4	32·0
1–2	28·3	28·4	28·9	26·6	27·0
3–5	15·9	17·3	15·5	17·9	16·8
6–11	14·9	11·9	11·9	17·1	15·0
12 +	5·5	4·6	9·1	9·0	9·0
Total	100·0	100·0	100·0	100·0	100·0

[a] In the UK there are no under-sixteen-year-olds eligible for full-time employment.

Source: European Labour Force Sample Survey.

For women, the results for West Germany and the UK are broadly similar to those for men, although there is a very evident tendency for the average duration of search to be lower for women than for men. The results for Italy are remarkable in that, while the average duration of search of teenage girls reflects that of the female working population as a whole, the average duration of search is exceptionally high for young women: in 1973 84 per cent of twenty- to twenty-four-year-old female job-seekers had been searching for six months or more and 51 per cent for a year or more. A possible explanation is that these are young women in poor households where other members either have low-income jobs or are themselves unemployed. They are seeking work to supplement the family income, but employers are reluctant to offer work, because of the high risk that they will quit in order to raise a family.

The three countries exhibit very different trends between 1973 and 1975. In West Germany the average duration of search lengthened, in Italy it changed very little, and in the UK it appears to have fallen. This last result is rather surprising, because the unemployment rate in the UK rose quite substantially, which means that the average duration of search should have increased too. The explanation seems to be the rapidly worsening employment situation in the UK during 1975, which meant that at the time of the survey a large number of people had only just lost their jobs. Between 1975 and 1977 the average duration of search appears to have lengthened again, because those made redundant in 1975 have failed to find new employment.[4]

The average duration of search for young people has tended to change in step with the average duration of search for the working population as a whole. Thus, in West Germany, the proportion of teenage boys who have been searching for more than a year rose sharply, from 4 per cent in 1973 to 11 per cent in 1975; in Italy it fell slightly, from 36 per cent in 1973 to 31 per cent in 1975; and in the UK it fell sharply, from 17 per cent to 6 per cent.

Changes in the average duration of job search by women have generally reflected those for men. The main differences are that in Italy the average duration of search of teenagers has fallen much more, while in the UK it has fallen less.

5.3   TRANSITIONS INTO AND OUT OF UNEMPLOYMENT

Table 5.2 classifies the unemployed according to their status a year

TABLE 5.2 STATUS A YEAR PREVIOUSLY. Unemployment rates according to status a year previously, together with the percentage of unemployed who are first-job seekers, by age group, 1973 and 1975

(a) West Germany: men

	Age group, 1973				Age group, 1975			
	Under 18	18–24	25–34	All ages	Under 18	18–24	25–34	All ages
Percentage unemployment among								
total working population	2·6	0·5	0·3	0·3	4·5	4·4	2·8	2·4
ex-services personnel	–	0·3	–	–	–	5·9	2·2	5·6
ex-students	3·4	3·7	2·4	3·4	9·9	8·9	12·4	10·0
previously seeking first job	3·1	7·5	16·9	21·1	34·2	50·0	40·4	45·4
previously unemployed	3·2	18·3	13·2	21·6	34·1	47·4	47·7	49·4
Percentage of unemployed who are first-job seekers	a	22·3	16·7	19·7	76·8	16·3	5·8	10·8

a Cannot be accurately estimated.

(b) Italy: men

	Age group, 1973				Age group, 1975			
	Under 18	18–24	25–34	All ages	Under 18	18–24	25–34	All ages
Percentage unemployment among								
total working population	17·1	10·8	2·6	2·7	13·5	8·6	2·3	2·1
ex-services personnel	–	21·2	28·1	21·6	–	21·8	37·5	23·2
ex-students	38·9	47·2	57·3	44·5	21·4	37·5	43·8	33·4
previously seeking first job	50·2	66·7	68·4	63·1	45·4	59·1	63·9	57·6
previously unemployed	49·5	62·7	54·7	55·4	42·1	53·6	51·2	47·9
Percentage of unemployed who are first-job seekers	95·4	74·0	56·6	57·1	93·0	74·8	50·4	55·8

(c) UK: men

	Age group, 1973				Age group, 1975			
	Under 18	*18–24*	*25–34*	*All ages*	*Under 18*	*18–24*	*25–34*	*All ages*
Percentage unemployment among total working population	5·0	3·2	2·2	2·2	5·2	6·8	3·7	3·8
ex-services personnel	–	–	–	–	–	–	–	–
ex-students	5·7	3·7	6·8	4·8	13·2	9·6	10·7	11·5
previously seeking first job	27·4	42·9	5·0	40·3	28·6	44·1	48·1	55·3
previously unemployed	35·2	33·5	35·4	44·0	16·7	43·3	47·8	55·0
Percentage of unemployed who are first-job seekers	41·8	7·8	1·8	4·0	60·8	8·6	3·2	5·5

(d) West Germany: women

	Age group, 1973				Age group, 1975			
	Under 18	*18–24*	*25–34*	*All ages*	*Under 18*	*18–24*	*25–34*	*All ages*
Percentage unemployed among total working population	0·6	0·5	0·5	0·5	7·7	3·1	2·9	2·6
ex-services personnel	–	–	–	–	–	–	–	–
ex-students	4·4	3·4	–	3·9	12·6	10·0	10·2	11·5
previously seeking first job	10·1	10·7	20·2	18·4	42·1	38·0	44·5	45·1
previously unemployed	7·7	16·6	22·2	19·6	56·8	43·1	48·4	48·7
Percentage of unemployed who are first-job seekers	a	25·2	4·1	19·9	89·5	18·9	6·4	16·3

a Cannot be accurately estimated.

(e) Italy: women

	Age group, 1973				Age group, 1975			
	Under 18	18–24	25–34	All ages	Under 18	18–24	25–34	All ages
Percentage unemployment among total working population	17·7	10·6	4·3	4·6	11·9	9·0	3·2	3·3
ex-services personnel	—	—	—	—	—	—	—	—
ex-students	31·4	57·5	52·0	45·6	35·6	45·4	56·1	41·3
previously seeking first job	47·7	67·5	53·8	63·1	34·7	60·3	62·2	56·0
previously unemployed	47·4	64·4	66·6	38·7	32·9	56·3	53·6	50·8
Percentage of unemployed who are first-job seekers	98·1	83·7	63·1	71·7	100·0	80·4	64·9	70·7

(f) UK: women

	Age group, 1973				Age group, 1975			
	Under 18	18–24	25–34	All ages	Under 18	18–24	25–34	All ages
Percentage unemployment among total working population	3·2	2·1	1·9	1·3	7·1	5·9	4·6	3·5
ex-services personnel	—	—	—	—	—	—	—	—
ex-students	4·1	3·2	9·3	3·9	13·2	5·9	13·2	10·0
previously seeking first job	36·2	24·6	44·8	38·3	27·3	40·8	63·0	56·4
previously unemployed	26·4	27·9	43·8	37·8	27·3	39·4	58·1	51·1
Percentage of unemployed who are first-job seekers	41·1	13·3	4·6	8·0	51·7	7·4	1·2	4·7

Source: European Labour Force Sample Survey.

previously. It shows how the current unemployment rate varies according to the previous status of the unemployed. The unemployment rate is calculated with reference to those who were in the working population at the time of the survey. It therefore excludes those who entered the workforce during the past year but retired from it before the survey was taken, because they could not find a job. On the other hand, it includes many who have only recently entered the working population.

The numbers on which the percentages are based are relatively small, so the effect of sampling errors may be quite considerable; this applies particularly to those who were unemployed a year ago, and even more to those who were seeking their first job.

It is evident that the proportion of first-job seekers among the unemployed is highest among young people, and declines steadily with age. This is true in each country, in both years and for both sexes.

The proportion of first-job seekers is particularly high in Italy: for example, for men in 1973 the proportion is 95 per cent for the under-eighteens, 74 per cent for the eighteen- to twenty-four-year-olds, and 57 per cent for the working population as a whole; for women the corresponding proportions are 98, 84 and 72 per cent, respectively. The statistics for 1975 are broadly similar.

In West Germany the proportion of first-job seekers among the unemployed is more moderate: the figures for 1973 are 22 per cent of unemployed men and 25 per cent of unemployed women in the eighteen to twenty-four age group, and 20 per cent of unemployed men and women in the working population as a whole. For 1975 the figures are lower: 16 and 19 per cent for men and women in the eighteen to twenty-four age group and 11 and 17 per cent for the working population as a whole.

In the UK the proportion of first-job seekers among the unemployed is relatively low. The situation of the under-eighteens may be distorted by the raising of the school-leaving age in 1972–3, although the statistics for the under-eighteens do not seem to be very much out of line with those for other age groups. In 1973 42 per cent of unemployed boys and 41 per cent of unemployed girls under eighteen were first-job seekers. The corresponding figures for eighteen- to twenty-four-year-olds are 8 and 13 per cent, while for the working population as a whole the figures fall to 4 and 7 per cent, respectively. By 1975 the situation was marginally worse for men and marginally better for women.

In West Germany and the UK there is little difference between the rate of unemployment among those who were seeking their first job a year ago and the rate of unemployment among the previously unemployed as a whole. However, in Italy unemployment among those previously seeking their first job is relatively high: for men in 1973 it was 63 per cent, as compared with 55 per cent for the unemployed as a whole, and for women 63, as compared with 39 per cent. In 1975 the corresponding figures were 58 and 48 per cent for men and 56 and 51 per cent for women.

In West Germany and Italy, unemployment rates among ex-service personnel increased significantly between 1973 and 1975, relative to the working population as a whole. Whereas in 1973 the unemployment rate in the eighteen to twenty-four age group in West Germany was only 0·3 per cent, in 1975 it was 6 per cent; while in Italy it increased marginally, from 21 to 22 per cent, at a time when the overall rate of unemployment fell.

Unemployment among ex-students (i.e. school-leavers and college graduates) is much higher than among ex-servicemen, and well above the average for the working population as a whole; on the other hand, it is much lower than unemployment among the previously unemployed. This is true for men in all three countries, and for women in all countries except Italy.

5.4 REASONS FOR JOB LOSS

Table 5.3 analyses job loss in different age groups. These statistics need to be interpreted with caution, since they reflect only the employee's account of how a job was lost. It is well known that employers and employees often disagree over whether a separation was owing to dismissal or resignation, particularly where the separation occurred at short notice.

A further qualification concerns the Italian statistics. In 1973 a large proportion of the Italian unemployed described themselves as formerly self-employed. This probably reflects the large amount of rural unemployment in Italy, particularly in the south. There are many agricultural smallholdings, and people with poor job prospects may work for the family on the smallholding; so far as the family is concerned they are self-employed. In fact those classified as 'self-employed' in Italy would perhaps be best considered simply as never having had full-time employment outside the household. Suitable adjustments were made to the 1975 survey.

TABLE 5.3   JOB LOSS.   Percentage of job losses attributable to various causes,
for selected age groups, 1973 and 1975

(a) West Germany: men

Cause of job loss	Age group						
	14–15	*16–19*	*14–19*	*20–24*	*25–29*	*30–34*	*All ages*
1973							
Dismissal	–	42·7	42·7	69·9	44·2	42·1	57·2
Resignation	–	57·3	57·3	30·1	55·8	47·0	37·8
Retirement	–	–	–	–	–	–	1·7
Ex self- employed	–	–	–	–	–	10.9	3.3
Total	–	100·0	100·0	100·0	100·0	100·0	100·0
1975							
Dismissal	–	91·3	91·3	87·5	86·5	89·8	88·7
Resignation	–	8·0	8·0	10·6	13·0	7·9	8·9
Retirement	–	0·7	0·7	0·4	–	2·3	1·0
Ex self- employed	–	–	–	1·5	0·5	–	1·4
Total	–	100·0	100·0	100·0	100·0	100·0	100·0

(b) Italy: men

Cause of job loss	Age group						
	14–15	*16–19*	*14–19*	*20–24*	*25–29*	*30–34*	*All ages*
1973							
Dismissal	41·2	41·4	41·4	54·5	58·9	70·9	66·1
Resignation	–	13·0	11·8	9·9	18·9	6·5	9·4
Retirement	–	–	–	–	–	–	–
Ex self- employed	58·8	45·6	46·8	35·6	22·2	22·6	24·6
Total	100·0	100·0	100·0	100·0	100·0	100·0	100·0
1975							
Dismissal	44·1	74·7	72·2	70·8	88·5	65·0	76·9
Resignation	55·9	23·1	25·8	29·0	7·1	17·4	10·0
Retirement	–	–	–	–	1·8	1·1	1·0
Ex self- employed	–	2·2	2·0	0·2	2·6	16·5	7·1
Total	100·0	100·0	100·0	100·0	100·0	100·0	100·0

(c) UK: men

Cause of job loss	Age group				
	14–19	*20–24*	*25–29*	*30–34*	*All ages*
1973					
Dismissal	57·4	70·7	62·9	70·4	70·4
Resignation	42·6	28·7	32·7	28·4	24·5
Retirement	–	0·6	0·6	–	2·3
Ex self-employed	–	–	3·8	1·2	2·8
Total	100·0	100·0	100·0	100·0	100·0
1975					
Dismissal	59·1	53·7	58·8	66·9	62·3
Resignation	39·3	45·2	36·3	24·8	28·2
Retirement	0·7	–	–	0·6	5·7
Ex self-employed	0·9	1·1	4·9	7·7	3·8
Total	100·0	100·0	100·0	100·0	100·0

(d) West Germany: women

Cause of job loss	Age group						
	14–15	*16–19*	*14–19*	*20–24*	*25–29*	*30–34*	*All ages*
1973							
Dismissal	–	36·8	36·8	27·4	17·8	55·2	46·6
Resignation	–	63·2	63·2	72·6	73·8	38·1	53·5
Retirement	–	–	–	–	–	–	2·6
Ex self-employed	–	–	–	–	8·4	6·7	2·3
Total	–	100·0	100·0	100·0	100·0	100·0	100·0
1975							
Dismissal	100·0	83·0	81·5	68·1	74·6	81·9	80·5
Resignation	–	16·7	16·6	31·2	24·0	17·2	18·4
Retirement	–	–	–	–	0·7	–	0·3
Ex self-employed	–	2·0	1·9	0·7	0·7	0·9	0·8
Total	100·0	100·0	100·0	100·0	100·0	100·0	100·0

(e) Italy: women

Cause of job loss	Age group						
	14–15	16–19	14–19	20–24	25–29	30–34	All ages
1973							
Dismissal	40·0	68·4	67·9	51·7	53·8	53·2	63·5
Resignation	–	5·4	5·3	12·3	5·9	14·9	8·2
Retirement	–	–	–	–	–	–	–
Ex self-employed	60·0	26·2	26·8	36·0	40·3	31·9	28·3
Total	100·0	100·0	100·0	100·0	100·0	100·0	100·0
1975							
Dismissal	100·0	74·0	74·4	82·0	69·6	80·2	79·8
Resignation	–	21·4	21·9	11·2	30·4	15·4	16·2
Retirement	–	4·6	4·5	–	–	–	0·6
Ex self-employed	–	–	–	6·8	–	4·4	3·4
Total	100·0	100·0	100·0	100·0	100·0	100·0	100·0

(f) UK: women

Cause of job loss	Age group				
	14–19	20–24	25–29	30–34	All ages
1973					
Dismissal	39·7	27·6	23·7	30·3	35·3
Resignation	60·3	71·1	76·3	69·7	60·1
Retirement	–	–	–	–	3·0
Ex self-employed	–	1·3	–	–	1·7
Total	100·0	100·0	100·0	100·0	100·0
1975					
Dismissal	47·7	33·6	31·4	37·6	43·9
Resignation	51·4	65·8	65·1	59·7	51·8
Retirement	–	–	0·8	2·7	2·7
Ex self-employed	0·9	0·6	2·7	–	1·6
Total	100·0	100·0	100·0	100·0	100·0

Source: European Labour Force Sample Survey.

Subject to these qualifications, the evidence suggests that resignations are particularly common among teenage boys, while dismissals are most common among twenty- to twenty-four-year-olds. The difference between teenagers and young adults is particularly marked in West Germany and the UK, and more so in 1973 than in 1975. In 1975 dismissals were a major factor in job losses for all age groups.

In 1973, 57 per cent of job losses by teenage boys in West Germany were owing to resignation, compared to 38 per cent for the working population as a whole. In Italy the figures were 12 and 9 per cent, respectively, and in the UK 43 and 24 per cent. In the same year 70 per cent of job losses by twenty- to twenty-four-year-old men in West Germany were owing to dismissal, but the corresponding figure for the working population as a whole is only 57 per cent. For the UK the figures were 29 and 24 per cent, respectively. In Italy the pattern was different: whereas 54 per cent of young mens' job losses were owing to dismissal, for the working population as a whole the figure is 66 per cent.

By 1975 any differences between teenage boys and young men had largely disappeared. Nearly 90 per cent of all job losses in West Germany were owing to dismissal, whatever the age group, while in Italy the figure was about 75 per cent. In the UK, resignations by young men increased dramatically, from 29 to 45 per cent, surpassing the percentage for teenage boys. (However, figures given in Table 5.4 suggest that risk of redundancy was a growing factor in resignations at this time.)

Among women the proportion of job losses accounted for by resignation tends to be higher than that for men. Resignations are much less important among teenage girls, and much more important among young women of twenty to twenty-four years old.

In 1973 63 per cent of job losses by teenage girls in West Germany were through resignation, as compared with 57 per cent for boys; while in the UK the figures were 60 and 43 per cent, respectively. For twenty- to twenty-four-year-olds, in West Germany the figures are 73 per cent for women and 30 per cent for men, and in the UK 71 per cent for women and 29 per cent for men. However, in Italy only 5 per cent of job losses by teenage girls were through resignation, as compared with 12 per cent for boys, while for twenty- to twenty-four-year-olds the proportion of resignations was higher: 12 per cent for women and 10 per cent for men.

5.5 REASONS FOR JOB SEARCH

Table 5.4 gives a breakdown of employed job-seekers by the reason for
their search. It indicates that dissatisfaction with present employment is
a more common reason for job search among teenagers than it is among
the working population as a whole. For example, in 1973 88 per cent of
teenage boys seeking jobs in West Germany were motivated by
dissatisfaction, while for the male working population as a whole the
figure is 86 per cent. In Italy the corresponding figures are 91 and 88 per
cent, and in the UK 91 and 86 per cent. Among women, the picture is
similar in Italy and the UK; the only exception is West Germany, where
85 per cent of teenage girls were motivated by dissatisfaction, compared
with 89 per cent for women as a whole.

For both teenage boys and young men the risk of redundancy is less
important than it is for other age groups. This is particularly true in
West Germany and the UK. For women it does not apply to the same
extent: risk of redundancy is a significant factor among teenage girls in
West Germany and twenty- to twenty-four-year-old women in Italy.

5.6 METHODS OF JOB SEARCH

Table 5.5 summarises the evidence on methods of job search. In West
Germany and Italy, where public employment agencies are the major
agency of job search, young workers make below-average use of them
and rely more on direct enquiry instead. On the other hand, in the UK,
where public employment exchanges are less used and more emphasis is placed on direct enquiry, young peoples' search behaviour
resembles that of other age groups.

Teenagers make relatively little use of journal advertisements as
compared with other groups, the only exception being in the case of
Italian women. However, this exception is hardly significant, since in
Italy on average only 1 per cent of women's jobs are sought by this
method.

In other respects young peoples' strategy of job search is not
noticeably different from that of other workers.

Between 1973 and 1975 the use of public employment agencies
increased markedly in West Germany, probably reflecting the declining
number of vacancies and the consequent need to use all avenues of
search, even those which do not normally lead to the best jobs. The role
of public agencies also increased in the UK, particularly among the

TABLE 5.4 REASON FOR SEARCH. Percentage distribution of employed persons seeking another job, by reason for search, for selected age groups, 1973 and 1975

(a) West Germany: men

Reason for search	Age group				
	14–19	*20–24*	*25–29*	*30–34*	*All ages*
1973					
Risk of redundancy	5·5	–	2·7	6·9	4·2
Dissatisfaction	88·5	84·7	90·9	81·5	85·6
Other	6·0	15·3	6·4	11·7	10·4
Total	100·0	100·0	100·0	100·0	100·0
1975					
Risk of redundancy	5·4	9·8	16·6	14·5	13·4
Dissatisfaction	72·9	66·6	70·7	69·7	71·9
Other	21·6	23·6	12·6	15·8	14·7
Total	100·0	100·0	100·0	100·0	100·0

(b) Italy: men

Reason for search	Age group				
	14–19	*20–24*	*25–29*	*30–34*	*All ages*
1973					
Risk of redundancy	7·0	9·0	9·5	5·3	8·9
Dissatisfaction	91·5	89·9	87·3	90·8	88·5
Other[a]	1·5	1·0	3·2	3·9	2·6
Total	100·0	100·0	100·0	100·0	100·0
1975					
Risk of redundancy	22·0	20·3	23·6	23·2	24·8
Dissatisfaction	78·0	79·6	76·4	76·7	75·2
Other[a]	–	–	–	–	–
Total	100·0	100·0	100·0	100·0	100·0

[a] The figures for 'Other' include those respondents who did not answer this question.

(c) UK: men

Reason for search	*Age group*				
	14–19	*20–24*	*25–29*	*30–34*	*All ages*
1973					
Risk of redundancy	5·7	6·4	7·7	8·6	9·8
Dissatisfaction	91·0	89·7	89·6	89·6	86·5
Other	3·4	3·8	2·7	2·7	3·7
Total	100·0	100·0	100·0	100·0	100·0
1975					
Risk of redundancy	10·7	13·4	15·8	14·6	16·3
Dissatisfaction	86·3	81·0	79·3	79·6	78·1
Other	3·0	5·6	5·0	5·8	5·6
Total	100·0	100·0	100·0	100·0	100·0

(d) West Germany: women

Reason for search	*Age group*				
	14–19	*20–24*	*25–29*	*30–34*	*All ages*
1973					
Risk of redundancy	12·3	3·9	2·5	2·6	4·6
Dissatisfaction	84·7	88·1	89·7	94·5	89·5
Other	3·0	8·0	7·8	2·9	6·0
Total	100·0	100·0	100·0	100·0	100·0
1975					
Risk of redundancy	9·1	5·5	5·7	–	7·6
Dissatisfaction	81·8	67·4	79·1	86·3	79·2
Other	9·1	27·1	15·3	13·7	13·2
Total	100·0	100·0	100·0	100·0	100·0

(e) Italy: women

Reason for search	Age group				
	14–19	*20–24*	*25–29*	*30–34*	*All ages*
1973					
Risk of redundancy	6·1	14·3	11·9	12·9	10·5
Dissatisfaction	93·4	84·2	87·0	83·0	87·9
Other[a]	0·5	1·5	1·1	4·1	1·7
Total	100·0	100·0	100·0	100·0	100·0
1975					
Risk of redundancy	24·7	24·6	22·5	25·2	24·5
Dissatisfaction	75·3	74·9	76·9	74·9	71·9
Other[a]	–	0·6	0·6	–	3·6
Total	100·0	100·0	100·0	100·0	100·0

[a] The figures for 'Other' include those respondents who did not answer this question.

(f) UK: women

Reason for search	Age group				
	14–19	*20–24*	*25–29*	*30–34*	*All ages*
1973					
Risk of redundancy	7·4	5·8	10·5	5·3	7·8
Dissatisfaction	89·7	92·0	82·2	86·4	86·2
Other	2·9	2·2	7·3	8·3	6·0
Total	100·0	100·0	100·0	100·0	100·0
1975					
Risk of redundancy	8·4	7·3	12·2	15·2	14·3
Dissatisfaction	89·1	85·7	76·9	68·5	76·5
Other	2·5	7·0	10·9	16·2	9·2
Total	100·0	100·0	100·0	100·0	100·0

Source: European Labour Force Sample Survey.

TABLE 5.5 METHOD OF SEARCH. Percentage distribution of job seekers by method of job search, for selected age groups, 1973 and 1975

(a) West Germany: men

Method of search	Age group				
	14–19	*20–24*	*25–29*	*30–34*	*All ages*
1973					
Public employment agency	42·6	38·1	42·9	31·2	49·8
Private employment agency	10·6	14·5	6·6	12·4	9·5
Journal advertisement	1·9	9·0	19·9	17·9	10·4
Direct enquiry	21·8	23·0	13·6	13·4	13·3
Personal contact	19·4	7·3	11·7	18·7	11·9
Other	3·6	7·6	5·3	6·3	5·0
Total	100·0	100·0	100·0	100·0	100·0
1975					
Public employment agency	77·4	86·4	77·2	78·9	83·1
Private employment agency	7·5	3·9	6·8	6·0	4·8
Journal advertisement	2·9	3·6	6·0	4·1	3·7
Direct enquiry	7·4	3·5	4·6	5·4	3·8
Personal contact	3·5	1·8	2·9	4·4	3·2
Other	1·0	0·8	2·5	1·2	1·4
Total	100·0	100·0	100·0	100·0	100·0

(b) Italy: men

Method of search	Age group				
	14–19	*20–24*	*25–29*	*30–34*	*All ages*
1973					
Public employment agency	39·5	38·3	32·0	39·6	40·2
Private employment agency	0·7	1·3	1·4	0·4	1·0
Journal advertisement	0·3	0·6	1·2	0·1	0·7
Direct enquiry	12·1	15·1	17·7	10·0	11·5
Personal contact	27·1	28·2	30·8	32·5	29·4
Other	20·2	16·4	16·8	17·4	17·2
Total	100·0	100·0	100·0	100·0	100·0
1975					
Public employment agency	41·9	47·8	44·0	48·0	47·7
Private employment agency	0·9	0·4	0·2	0·1	0·4
Journal advertisement	0·6	0·5	0·6	0·5	0·5
Direct enquiry	6·7	5·2	8·1	7·8	6·2
Personal contact	22·5	11·9	9·6	16·0	16·6
Other	27·4	34·2	37·5	27·6	28·6
Total	100·0	100·0	100·0	100·0	100·0

(c) UK: men

Method of search	Age group				
	14–19	*20–24*	*25–29*	*30–34*	*All ages*
1973					
Public employment agency	31·9	29·0	21·6	26·7	34·0
Private employment agency	2·0	2·8	2·3	2·1	2·0
Journal advertisement	1·6	3·3	2·7	1·8	2·3
Direct enquiry	34·6	44·4	53·2	47·9	41·4
Personal contact	6·4	5·9	5·6	8·6	7·0
Other	23·6	14·6	14·5	12·8	13·7
Total	100·0	100·0	100·0	100·0	100·0
1975					
Public employment agency	40·2	38·8	27·0	33·2	39·4
Private employment agency	1·6	3·0	4·3	3·1	2·5
Journal advertisement	2·4	2·9	8·1	3·4	2·5
Direct enquiry	31·0	42·5	54·0	50·3	42·2
Personal contact	4·1	4·0	5·3	4·7	5·2
Other	20·7	8·8	6·3	5·3	8·2
Total	100·0	100·0	100·0	100·0	100·0

(d) West Germany: women

Method of search	Age group				
	14–19	*20–24*	*25–29*	*30–34*	*All ages*
1973					
Public employment agency	39·5	42·3	39·1	45·5	50·6
Private employment agency	19·4	10·6	17·4	12·1	12·4
Journal advertisement	4·5	24·8	14·7	12·8	11·9
Direct enquiry	23·5	12·3	8·8	14·3	11·6
Personal contact	10·5	5·1	10·0	7·0	7·9
Other	2·7	4·9	10·0	7·2	5·5
Total	100·0	100·0	100·0	100·0	100·0
1975					
Public employment agency	70·3	76·3	79·6	75·6	77·8
Private employment agency	6·9	5·8	5·1	5·3	5·0
Journal advertisement	4·8	5·6	7·0	8·4	5·9
Direct enquiry	11·5	6·6	3·9	2·2	5·2
Personal contact	5·4	2·5	2·0	4·8	3·6
Other	1·1	3·2	2·4	3·7	2·5
Total	100·0	100·0	100·0	100·0	100·0

(e) Italy: women

Method of search	Age group				
	14–19	*20–24*	*25–29*	*30–34*	*All ages*
1973					
Public employment agency	27·9	25·0	28·2	29·0	29·8
Private employment agency	0·3	0·7	0·4	0·9	0·5
Journal advertisement	0·8	1·0	0·3	0·5	0·7
Direct enquiry	16·1	18·2	17·4	10·8	14·7
Personal contact	29·7	26·2	27·3	30·0	28·7
Other	25·2	28·8	26·4	28·8	25·8
Total	100·0	100·0	100·0	100·0	100·0
1975					
Public employment agency	36·6	35·1	34·7	40·8	37·6
Private employment agency	0·5	0·6	0·2	0·4	0·4
Journal advertisement	1·1	1·1	0·7	2·0	1·1
Direct enquiry	8·3	6·4	4·9	6·1	6·6
Personal contact	25·8	16·0	16·7	18·3	21·1
Other	27·7	40·8	42·8	32·4	33·2
Total	100·0	100·0	100·0	100·0	100·0

(f) UK: women

Method of search	Age group				
	14–19	*20–24*	*25–29*	*30–34*	*All ages*
1973					
Public employment agency	18·9	13·7	11·1	9·8	13·0
Private employment agency	6·5	7·4	6·0	5·3	5·5
Journal advertisement	2·3	2·4	4·3	3·2	3·2
Direct enquiry	45·5	50·1	60·9	61·5	54·8
Personal contact	6·0	5·9	3·9	5·9	5·6
Other	20·9	20·4	13·7	14·4	17·9
Total	100·0	100·0	100·0	100·0	100·0
1975					
Public employment agency	26·5	19·0	11·5	9·6	15·7
Private employment agency	6·5	7·6	7·2	5·5	6·2
Journal advertisement	2·6	4·3	4·5	5·0	4·4
Direct enquiry	43·5	56·1	67·2	65·8	59·6
Personal contact	4·0	4·4	3·2	6·3	4·3
Other	16·9	8·6	6·4	7·8	9·8
Total	100·0	100·0	100·0	100·0	100·0

Source: European Labour Force Sample Survey.

young; this may be owing in part to a shortage of vacancies for young people, but it could also reflect the changing image of the employment service associated with the introduction of high-street Job Centres.

To some extent the data in Table 5.5 mask significant differences between the different categories of job-seeker in the strategy of job search. The unemployed rely more heavily on the public employment agencies than do those already in employment. People with jobs – and to a lesser extent first-job seekers – rely much more on informal methods of search, such as direct enquiry and personal contact.[5]

5.7 INDUSTRIAL DISTRIBUTION OF THE WORKING POPULATION

Table 5.6 shows the distribution of employment among industries for various age groups. It is useful to consider each industry in turn.

The proportion of workers aged between fourteen and thirty-four employed in agriculture is relatively low: thus the agricultural workforce tends to be older than average. However, in Italy and the UK the proportion of teenagers employed in agriculture is significantly higher than the proportion of young adults.

Both in energy and water and in minerals there is little systematic relation between age and employment. In each country the age distributions for the two industries are broadly similar, but across countries there are considerable differences. On average the age distribution is approximately rectangular. However, there is a clear tendency for the proportion of teenagers employed in these industries to be low relative to the proportion of young adults.

With respect to engineering, the male workforce in West Germany and Italy is predominantly youthful, while for the female workforce no systematic pattern is discernible. In the UK the male workforce has an approximately rectangular age distribution.

It is quite clear that in the other manufacturing and construction industries the workforce is predominantly youthful. However, the most remarkable single feature of the data is undoubtedly the concentration of young people, particularly teenagers, in the distributive trades. For example, in West Germany 22 per cent of teenage boys are employed in distribution, compared with 13 per cent of the male working population as a whole, while in the UK the corresponding proportions are 22 and 14 per cent. The effect is not quite so pronounced for women, probably because a high proportion of women of all ages are employed in distribution anyway.

TABLE 5.6   BRANCH OF INDUSTRY.   Percentage distribution of employment by branch of industry, for selected age groups, 1975

(a) West Germany: men

Branch (NACE classification)	Age group				
	14–19	*20–24*	*25–29*	*30–34*	*All ages*
Agriculture	3·3	3·9	3·2	2·4	4·9
Energy and water	2·6	1·7	1·9	2·4	3·0
Minerals and chemicals	4·8	5·9	6·8	7·7	7·9
Engineering	26·1	21·1	23·1	22·6	21·0
Other manufacturing	10·4	9·9	10·7	10·4	10·9
Building/public works	15·5	10·9	11·7	12·0	11·4
Distribution and catering	21·6	15·8	13·3	12·6	12·7
Transport and communications	6·4	6·6	8·6	7·9	7·7
Banking and insurance	3·2	4·6	5·1	5·5	4·5
Government	3·9	16·6	9·2	8·5	9·6
Other services	2·2	3·6	6·4	8·0	6·4
Total	100·0	100·0	100·0	100·0	100·0

(b) Italy: men

Branch (NACE classification)	Age group				
	14–19	*20–24*	*25–29*	*30–34*	*All ages*
Agriculture	10·4	9·2	6·5	7·5	13·8
Energy and water	1·1	1·7	2·8	2·7	1·8
Minerals and chemicals	1·3	1·8	2·3	2·4	2·3
Engineering	23·1	20·2	17·1	14·2	12·9
Other manufacturing	31·3	27·5	23·1	20·4	13·9
Building/public works	14·4	14·7	13·0	13·0	12·8
Distribution and catering	13·8	11·5	10·8	12·0	12·3
Transport and communications	1·1	11·0	8·0	8·1	7·3
Banking and insurance	0·4	2·0	2·9	3·0	2·1
Government	0·2	1·7	4·2	6·2	6·2
Other services	2·9	0·7	9·3	10·5	9·6
Total	100·0	100·0	100·0	100·0	100·0

(c) UK: men

Branch (NACE classification)	Age group				
	14–19	*20–24*	*25–29*	*30–34*	*All ages*
Agriculture	3·5	3·2	2·7	3·1	3·6
Energy and water	3·7	3·6	4·0	4·2	4·7
Minerals and chemicals	5·4	6·1	6·3	6·8	6·6
Engineering	18·5	17·7	17·1	18·5	18·6
Other manufacturing	14·1	11·8	10·8	10·9	10·3
Building/public works	15·4	13·7	13·1	12·3	11·3
Distribution and catering	22·1	15·8	12·3	13·0	13·7
Transport and communications	4·5	6·8	8·3	7·8	8·4
Banking and insurance	4·3	7·2	8·0	6·5	5·7
Government	3·3	6·8	7·8	7·3	6·2
Other services	5·2	7·5	9·7	9·6	9·9
Total	100·0	100·0	100·0	100·0	100·0

(d) West Germany: women

Branch (NACE classification)	Age group				
	14–19	*20–24*	*25–29*	*30–34*	*All ages*
Agriculture	2·0	2·4	4·4	6·4	8·8
Energy and water	0·2	0·6	0·5	0·6	0·5
Minerals and chemicals	2·4	4·2	4·0	4·2	3·7
Engineering	8·2	11·8	13·7	11·4	11·1
Other manufacturing	15·1	14·0	14·1	13·3	14·0
Building/public works	1·7	1·7	1·6	2·5	1·7
Distribution and catering	31·0	21·5	18·5	22·7	22·8
Transport and communications	2·3	3·1	2·9	3·3	3·2
Banking and insurance	9·2	10·9	9·1	7·5	6·9
Government	5·4	5·6	7·1	6·7	7·4
Other services	22·5	21·2	24·1	21·4	20·1
Total	100·0	100·0	100·0	100·0	100·0

(e) Italy: women

Branch (NACE classification)	Age group				
	14–19	*20–24*	*25–29*	*30–34*	*All ages*
Agriculture	7·3	5·8	6·2	9·0	14·5
Energy and water	0·1	0·5	0·4	0·4	0·3
Minerals and chemicals	1·3	1·7	1·3	1·2	1·1
Engineering	8·9	8·1	7·7	6·0	5·5
Other manufacturing	45·6	38·6	32·4	25·5	26·5
Building/public works	1·0	0·8	0·6	0·5	0·4
Distribution and catering	19·2	12·6	14·8	17·0	18·6
Transport and communications	0·7	1·7	2·0	1·8	1·7
Banking and insurance	0·9	2·8	2·1	1·3	1·3
Government	0·8	2·4	4·6	4·9	3·5
Other services	14·2	20·9	27·9	32·4	26·6
Total	100·0	100·0	100·0	100·0	100·0

(f) UK: women

Branch (NACE classification)	Age group				
	14–19	*20–24*	*25–29*	*30–34*	*All ages*
Agriculture	0·7	0·6	0·8	1·3	1·6
Energy and water	1·2	1·6	1·1	0·8	1·1
Minerals and chemicals	4·3	3·3	3·1	2·3	2·9
Engineering	8·9	9·1	8·6	8·9	8·9
Other manufacturing	19·2	14·6	13·3	12·9	13·2
Building/public works	1·2	1·5	1·4	1·3	1·2
Distribution and catering	25·0	12·2	20·4	22·2	23·0
Transport and communications	3·0	3·7	3·1	2·9	3·0
Banking and insurance	14·3	14·4	10·0	6·8	7·3
Government	5·4	3·5	6·4	4·3	5·5
Other services	16·8	34·0	31·8	36·3	32·8
Total	100·0	100·0	100·0	100·0	100·0

Source: European Labour Force Sample Survey.

The transport and communications industry has a predominantly old labour force, and in particular employs a relatively small proportion of male teenagers.

In banking and insurance there is a clear tendency for the female working population to be predominantly youthful; the effect is more pronounced among young adults than among teenagers. The same effect, though slightly weaker, is also discernible among men.

In government there is a strong tendency for teenagers, both male and female, to be underrepresented in the workforce, while in the 'other services' sector this is true not only of teenagers but also of young adults.

6 Interpretation of the Evidence

6.1 INTRODUCTION

This chapter considers how the theories advanced in Chapter 4 can be used to interpret the evidence reported in the previous chapter. To a certain extent the intention is to test each of the theories against the EEC statistics. But, because of data limitations, it is not possible conclusively to accept or reject any of the theories. The main problem is that the results of two cross-section surveys at different points in time do not make it possible to build up a full picture of the dynamics of the labour market – the movement of people between jobs, into and out of the workforce, and so on. Much of the evidence therefore bears only indirectly on the crucial question of how the youth labour market functions. Thus all that can be done is to select those hypotheses which appear most useful in explaining the predominant features of the current youth-unemployment situation. These hypotheses are used in the next chapter to appraise alternative policies for youth employment.

The organisation of the chapter follows that of Cnapter 4. Sections 6.2–6.6 are concerned with explanations of the relatively high incidence of unemployment among young people. Sections 6.7 and 6.8 are concerned with cyclical instability, while section 6.9 is concerned with the long-term trend. The conclusions are briefly summarised in section 6.10.

6.2 JOB-SEARCH HYPOTHESIS

The evidence is very much in favour of the job-search hypothesis. This hypothesis is concerned with less able young workers who have just entered working life and are still economically dependent on their parents. As such, the hypothesis is principally concerned with teenage unemployment.

Its first and most important prediction is that young people change jobs fairly frequently. A comparison of the unemployment rates in Table 1.1 with the duration-of-search data in Table 5.1 clearly indicates that high unemployment among young people cannot possibly be attributed to a long duration of search; this suggests that the explanation lies in a high frequency of job-changing. Direct confirmation is difficult to obtain from the EEC data, but there are other sources which provide corroboration. For example, the General Household Survey of the UK indicates that in 1973, 24 per cent of boys and girls under eighteen, and the same proportion of young people aged eighteen to twenty-four, changed employers at least once a year, while only 20 per cent in the twenty-five to thirty-four and 13 per cent in the thirty-five to forty-four age group did.[1] There is an even greater disparity in the job-changing habits of different age groups in 1975. Thus, the first prediction of the job-search theory appears to be strongly confirmed.

The second prediction is that resignations are a much more common reason for job loss among young workers. Table 5.3 supports this prediction as far as teenagers are concerned, but suggests that the opposite may be true for young adults.

Table 5.4 corroborates the third prediction – that dissatisfaction with their present job is a major factor in teenagers' job search. It is instructive to consider this view in the light of evidence for the UK that job satisfaction is relatively high among young workers under eighteen (see Table 6.1). The inference must be that young workers do not change jobs more frequently because they are more dissatisfied with their jobs than other workers are, but that the minority who are dissatisfied are more likely to change jobs when young than they are when older. This confirms the view that the opportunity cost of job-changing is much lower for young workers.

The final prediction, that young people use informal methods of job search, receives only limited support from Table 5.5. It is difficult to draw very firm conclusions, because of the sharp change in the pattern of job search between 1973 and 1975.

Subject to this qualification, it appears that the predictions of the job-search theory are borne out quite well by the evidence on teenage unemployment. But, as expected, the theory does not work well in explaining unemployment among young adults.

TABLE 6.1   Job satisfaction according to age, UK 1973

Age	*Degree of job satisfaction*					
	Very satisfied (score 5)	*Fairly satisfied (score 4)*	*Neither satisfied nor dissatisfied (score 3)*	*Rather dissatisfied (score 2)*	*Very dissatisfied (score 1)*	*Average Score*
	%	%	%	%	%	
1973						
Under 18	42	45	9	4	1	4·2
18–24	36	44	11	6	4	4·0
25–34	39	45	8	5	3	4·1
35–44	42	44	7	5	2	4·2
1975						
Under 18	55	32	5	6	3	4·3
18–24	37	44	6	8	4	4·0
25–34	40	41	6	9	4	4·0
35–44	43	43	5	7	3	4·2

Source: Office of Population Censuses and Surveys, *General Household Survey 1973* (London: HMSO, 1975), Table 3.2, and *General Household Survey 1975* (London: HMSO, 1977), Table 5.3.

6.3 SEASONAL-UNEMPLOYMENT HYPOTHESIS

The evidence suggests that young people constitute a relatively high proportion of the workforce in certain seasonal and casual trades. However, direct confirmation of the seasonality of youth unemployment is difficult to obtain, since monthly time series are not available. The only information concerns school-leavers, where the seasonal influences simply reflect the timing of school-leaving, at the end of each term and at the end of the academic year.[2] It must, therefore, remain a matter for conjecture whether the concentration of young people in seasonal and casual trades exerts a significant influence on youth unemployment as a whole.

The proportion of young people in various industries is summarised in Table 5.6, which indicates that young people are well represented in engineering, other manufacturing, building and public works ('construction'), and distribution and catering. Neither engineering nor other manufacturing exhibits any marked seasonality in production, but there does appear to be a seasonal element in construction and in distribution and catering.[3] The seasonal element in construction is due to the influence of the weather, while in distribution and catering the influence of tourism is almost certainly paramount.

Construction also qualifies as a casual trade, because the work is typically organised around short-term projects for which labour is recruited on a day-to-day or week-to-week basis. If labour turnover is used as an index of the casualness of employment, then distribution and catering, and certain trades in other manufacturing – notably timber, clothing and textiles – also qualify as casual.[4] To this extent it is legitimate to say that young people are concentrated in seasonal and casual trades.

This does not mean that all seasonal and casual trades employ a high proportion of young people. Agriculture is a seasonal trade where casual labour is important, yet the number of young people employed is relatively small. This probably reflects the post-war decline of the agricultural workforce, which has meant that there have been relatively few openings for young people.

The evidence on seasonal unemployment is very flimsy, and it is difficult to reach any conclusion other than that the concentration of young workers in construction and distribution may have some connection with a preference among young workers for seasonal and casual employment. Much more research needs to be done before the significance of seasonal and casual unemployment among young workers can be established.

6.4 LIFE-CYCLE HYPOTHESIS

The life-cycle hypothesis asserts that young people are concentrated in low-wage industries offering sociable working conditions, but where their long-term prospects are poor; unemployment arises when young people attempt to switch out of these industries in their late 'teens or early twenties in order to find higher-paid-work.

We have already seen that the age composition of the workforce varies considerably from industry to industry. This may be partly the effect of entry qualifications. Young People are underrepresented in transport and communication, banking and insurance, government, and other services. In transport and communication the need for responsibility leads to minimum age requirements for driving vehicles, and so forth, while in other cases the need for academic and professional qualifications restricts most jobs to sixth-form leavers or graduates.

These restrictions on entry force young people into other industries.

In West Germany and Italy a relatively high proportion enter engineering, but this does not apply in the UK. It appears that the growth of the engineering industry in West Germany and Italy has created job opportunities for young people, while in the UK the industry has remained relatively static. This is borne out by the fact that in West Germany and Italy wages in engineering are fairly high relative to other occupations, while in the UK they are low (see Table 6.2). Where craft unions insist that all entrants first qualify as apprentices, firms are forced to expand apprenticeships rather than recruit older skilled workers from other trades. However, the fact that the demand for labour is buoyant means that the young workers have secure prospects, and are unlikely to have to transfer out of the industry later on.

TABLE 6.2 Average gross hourly earnings in selected manufacturing industries, 1973 and 1975

Industry	Italy (Lire)		UK (pence)		West Germany (DM)	
	1973	1975	1973	1975	1973	1975
Mineral-oil refining	1515	2186	103·6	170·1	10·04	12·68
Iron and steel	1206	1855	97·7	156·5	9·24	10·72
Cement	1083	1592	89·6	149·4	9·04	10·17
Chemicals	1179	1728	83·9	136·6	8·37	10·51
Metal manufacturing	985	1483	81·8	126·2	8·09	9·71
Mechanical engineering	1042	1551	85·9	130·3	8·62	10·42
Electrical engineering	1007	1476	76·0	117·7	7·38	9·10
Motor vehicles	1089	1521	106·1	147·8	9·21	11·30
Food, drink and tobacco	946	1549	76·9	119·8	7·13	8·75
Textiles	748	1279	68·0	107·2	6·45	7·34
Clothing and footwear	671	1136	57·2	86·5	6·02	7·24
Paper, printing and publishing	1145	1745	93·9	138·5	8·33	9·97
Rubber and plastics	1012	1616	83·8	130·9	7·40	9·04
Other manufacturing	772	1266	68·2	104·0	7·82	8·21
Building & civil engineering	934	1454	84·4	129·0	8·61	9·89
All manufacturing	958	1490	82·1	125·8	7·94	9·68
All industries	956	1488	82·1	126·4	8·06	9·72[a]

[a] Estimated; source data incorrect.

Sources. All except UK 1973: Statistical Office of the European Communities, *Hourly Earning – Hours of Work*, no. 1, 1977, Tables 3, 5, 9. UK 1973: Statistical Office of the European Communities, *Social Statistics (Hourly Earnings)*, no. 2, 1975, Table 9.

Unfortunately, the same cannot be said of the other industries into which large numbers of young workers are recruited: construction, distribution and other manufacturing. It is certainly true that wages are fairly high in construction, but, as noted earlier, the work is casual and so income prospects are uncertain. This is unlikely to suit young adults acquiring new financial responsibilities. In both distribution and other manufacturing, wages tend to be very low, so that young people are obliged to switch out when they acquire a family to support.

The quality of training in these industries is known to be very poor. Although nominally there are many apprenticeships in construction, in practice these confer little training; their main role appears to be to justify higher rates of pay for certain groups of workers with 'craftsman' status.[5] In many branches of distribution, training is virtually non-existent, although where it is provided it may develop general business skills of considerable value in other trades.[6] It is difficult to generalise about the other-manufacturing sector, but it includes a number of trades – textiles, timber, and so on – where training opportunities are extremely limited. On the whole, therefore, it appears that when young people leave these trades they have little expertise to offer employers in other industries, and so are likely to find it difficult to obtain a job which satisfies their higher income aspirations.

The data in Table 5.6 suggest that young people move out into transport and communications, minerals and chemicals, and energy and water. It appears that they receive higher wages in return for less enjoyable working conditions and less sociable hours of work. The more skilled workers may be able to obtain work in banking, government and other services.

It is difficult to assess the extent to which young adults suffer unemployment as a result of moving from low-wage to high-wage industries. There is certainly no evidence that the duration of unemployment is particularly high among twenty- to twenty-four-year-olds. Without more data it cannot be established that voluntary movement out of unskilled trades is a major cause of unemployment among young adults.

6.5 QUEUE HYPOTHESIS

This hypothesis connects youth unemployment with redundancies inflicted on young workers who become eligible for adult wages. The wage may be a statutory minimum wage or may be negotiated by a union on the principle of maintaining a differential between apprentices and qualified craftsmen.

There is little doubt that in low-wage industries many workers receive no more than the statutory minimum. Statutory schemes usually implement strictly proportional differentials between youth and adult wages, with the discontinuities being most common at eighteen and at twenty-one. In low-wage industries the work is typically unskilled, so that productivity does not significantly increase with age or experience. It follows that the employer has a strong incentive to make young workers redundant when they become entitled to adult wages. Evidence from a number of countries suggests that employers in the distributive trades and in the miscellaneous-services sector are frequently in this position.[7]

The second line of argument concerns high-wage industries where, it is alleged, the craftsman receives an artificially high wage. This argument seems to have less justification now than it did previously. Technical change has forced craft unions to accept dilution, in the form of 'unqualified' men performing the same work as craftsmen; consequently differentials between 'skilled' and 'unskilled' manual workers have narrowed. This makes apprenticeship much less attractive to the young worker. At the same time, statutory obligations to release apprentices for formal education have increased the net cost of apprenticeship to the employer. As a result the number of apprentices has declined relative to the number of craftsmen. In some industries the number of apprentices is now so low that there are insufficient to maintain the skilled labour force at its existing level.[8] In these circumstances an employer has little incentive to make redundant a newly qualified craftsman.

One of the most obvious predictions of the queue hypothesis is that a high proportion of young adults will lose their jobs through dismissal. The data in Table 5.3 give only a weak indication of this; it seems to be true in some cases, but the pattern is by no means a consistent one.

A further prediction of the queue hypothesis is that the duration of unemployment among young adults will tend to be high, as they will wait around for the chance of a vacancy at adult rates. This does not seem to be borne out in practice: the average duration of unemployment, although greater than for teenagers, is still low compared with that for the working population as a whole. One reason may be that those dismissed from a trade where the statutory minimum wage prevails soon realise that the adult wage – although higher than the youth wage – is still relatively low compared with wages in other trades. The higher wage offered elsewhere soon induces the unemployed to change to less congenial work in other trades, rather than continue in unemployment.

On balance, therefore, it appears that the queue hypothesis does not explain very well either how young people come to lose their jobs, or how they behave once they have become unemployed.

6.6 BENEFIT-INDUCED UNEMPLOYMENT HYPOTHESIS

This is a controversial hypothesis and one which is notoriously difficult to test.

The usual formulation of the hypothesis is that the rate of unemployment is high when unemployment benefit is equivalent to a large proportion of the expected income from employment. It is usually tested at the aggregate level by correlating rates of unemployment and national rates of benefit, either at different times in the same country, or across different countries.

A straightforward comparison across countries lends little support to the hypothesis. Both West Germany and the UK offer much more generous unemployment benefit than Italy, yet until 1975 the rate of unemployment was highest in Italy. On the other hand, between 1973 and 1975, the unemployment situation deteriorated in both West Germany and the UK. Although there were major tax reforms in Germany in 1974–5, it seems unlikely that there could be such an immediate response. It is more likely that workers respond once they are unemployed, and have become familiar with the benefit system. The benefit system may then encourage them to become more selective in their choice of employment, and so prolong job search.

This is corroborated by the experience of the UK, which introduced earnings-related unemployment benefit in 1966. Since then there has been a shift in the relation between unemployment and vacancies, so that with a given number of vacancies there are now a larger number of unemployed. Of course, higher unemployment benefit may not be the only reason for this. It is possible that the introduction of redundancy payments, also in 1966, may have reduced workers' resistance to redundancy, and made it easier for firms to 'dishoard' employees. Firms may now accommodate short-term fluctuations in demand by hiring and firing workers (or varying overtime) rather than by adjusting the amount of 'slack' in labour utilisation. On this view it is firms' increased use of the labour market which has been responsible for the rises in the stocks of unemployment and vacancies. Redundancy payments may also have encouraged firms to 'shake out' inefficient older labour and to create new vacancies for prime-age workers with more modern skills. The mismatch between the redundant workers and the newly-created vacancies may have generated a structural problem in which the redundant workers remain unemployed and the skilled vacancies remain unfilled. Another possibility is that some of the unemployed have taken part-time work which they conceal from the authorities.

Notwithstanding this, there are strong grounds for believing that the introduction of earnings-related unemployment benefit has had some effect on the unemployment situation.[9] Unemployment benefit rose from about 49 per cent of average earnings in 1965 to nearly 69 per cent in 1966, and has risen even further since then. Survey results suggest that workers in receipt of benefit tend to stipulate higher money wages when applying for jobs, and take longer to find new jobs when made redundant. Econometric estimates based on aggregate data suggest that the introduction of the earnings-related supplement may have raised the unemployment rate by an average of 0·6 per cent over the period 1967–72. It appears, therefore, that at least part of the explanation is that the unemployed are prolonging job search because of the high level of unemployment benefit.

The application of the hypothesis to youth unemployment is based on the assumption that for young people the benefit constitutes a relatively high proportion of the average wage. In the UK it is the 'supplementary benefit' rather than unemployment benefit itself which is relevant to young workers.[10] Unemployment benefit is paid only to those with a certain level of previous employment experience. Those who quit their jobs are normally disqualified for six weeks; and, since most young unemployed lose their jobs by quitting and are then fairly quickly re-employed, they typically do not qualify even where their previous employment experience is adequate. Current scales of supplementary benefit tend to favour married men with dependants, so that for a low-paid prime age worker the supplementary benefit would be about two-thirds of his post-tax wage, while for a young dependant it would be unlikely to exceed one-third of the post-tax wage. Although the young worker does not have the same commitments as the older worker, it is clear that his loss of income is, in proportional terms, much greater.

Taking the UK system to be fairly typical of EEC countries, it appears that state subsidies to the unemployed are unlikely to account for the high rate of unemployment among young people. However, a broader interpretation of the benefit hypothesis includes the effects of subsidies which young people receive from their families. Unfortunately the data do not allow us to examine this effect. It would be interesting to have information on the incidence of unemployment among young people according to the size of the household, the number of other income-earners in the household, and so on. Until such data are available, a comprehensive test of the benefit-induced unemployment hypothesis will not be possible.

6.7 SCHOOL-LEAVER HYPOTHESIS

The school-leaver hypothesis is concerned mainly with unemployment during a recession. In terms of the data at our disposal, a recession may be diagnosed as a situation of high unemployment and prolonged job search. It is generally recognised that 1975 was a year of worldwide recession, although 1973 was also a year of high unemployment in Italy, and to a lesser extent in the UK. Between 1973 and 1975 the situation deteriorated considerably in West Germany, worsened in the UK, and improved somewhat in Italy.

The first prediction for the school-leaver hypothesis is that unemployment among ex-students will change in the same direction, but by a much greater margin, than unemployment among the working population as whole. Table 5.2 corroborates this exactly: between 1973 and 1975, unemployment among ex-students rose sharply in West Germany and the UK, and fell significantly in Italy.

The second prediction is that first-job seekers constitute a high proportion of the young unemployed. This is also borne out by Table 5.2, which shows that the proportion of first-job seekers among the unemployed is highest among the very young. However, these figures need to be interpreted with caution, since, as noted earlier, there is a significant seasonal element in the number of unemployed school-leavers, which may influence the statistics of unemployed first-job seekers.

The third prediction is that school-leavers are the most vulnerable group among the first-job seekers, and once again this is borne out by the evidence. For example, between 1973 and 1975 the proportion of first-job seekers among the unemployed actually fell in West Germany, although unemployment among ex-students increased; a similar reverse movement is also apparent among UK women. Only among the under-eighteen-year-olds is the behaviour of ex-students and first-job seekers similar, which is hardly surprising, since at this age the two groups are more or less identical.

The explanation suggested by the school-leaver hypothesis is that other potential entrants to the labour force are much more flexible, and find it easier to postpone entry to the working population if there is a serious risk of unemployment. As the recession deepens they are able to withdraw from the labour force, while potential school-leavers are not. Unfortunately, evidence on labour-force participation lends little support to this view. It suggests that the vulnerability of school-leavers is owing to other characteristics, which make them less competitive when seeking jobs.[11]

The decision to enter the workforce depends on a complex of factors, of which the chance of obtaining a good job is but one. Another factor is the need for an additional wage to supplement household income: the importance of this depends on the composition of the household and in particular on the number of other income-earners already in it. For potential school-leavers a further consideration is the expected financial return from obtaining higher educational qualifications by staying on at school.

In most European countries there has been a postwar trend for young people to prolong their education, and this is reflected in the declining labour-force participation of young people (see Table 6.3). This is probably owing to changing expectations regarding the value of educational qualifications. In some countries this trend has recently been arrested, or even reversed; for example, in the UK the number staying on at school beyond sixteen dropped sharply following the raising of the school-leaving age in 1973.[12] There has also been a trend for the labour-force participation of women to rise; the trend has been particularly strong among married women aged between twenty-five and forty. This may reflect the rising income aspirations of young couples, and may also be connected with the recent fall in the birth rate, which allows a higher proportion of young married women to go out to work.[13]

It is to be expected that the influence of unemployment will be superimposed on these trends. However, there is little evidence that between 1973 and 1975 there were substantial deviations from trend. Certainly the increasing participation of prime-age women does not seem to have been arrested, nor, at first sight, has the declining participation of young people. It is possible, though, that unemployment has had some effect on young people, because, in the absence of unemployment, the numbers staying on at school might have been expected to level off, owing to the diminishing value of graduate qualification.

TABLE 6.3 Percentage labour-force participation

Category	Age groups									
	14–19	*20–24*	*25–29*	*30–39*	*40–49*	*50–54*	*55–59*	*60–64*	*65–69*	*70 +*
1960										
W. Germany										
Men	72·1	90·5	96·1	98·0	96·5	94·0	88·5	71·4	31·1	15·2
Women	70·6	74·6	51·0	44·3	42·0	36·5	31·6	19·9	11·9	4·9
Italy										
Men	65·6	76·8	95·8	97·6	95·7	93·1	86·6	61·4	39·7	20·0
Women	45·4	48·7	36·9	34·3	33·2	30·2	24·2	17·7	11·7	4·7
1968										
W. Germany										
Men	50·3	85·6	93·9	98·6	97·6	94·6	89·9	75·7	33·2	13·1
Women	48·8	67·4	48·5	42·3	46·2	42·6	36·1	22·5	12·0	4·6
Italy										
Men	44·5	79·1	95·3	98·2	96·4	92·0	82·9	51·9	27·0	9·2
Women	30·9	42·9	31·8	28·8	30·2	25·7	18·3	12·7	6·2	1·8
1973										
W.Germany										
Men	39·4	80·8	91·0	98·3	98·0	93·9	87·5	70·4	25·1	7·8
Women	37·3	68·0	53·5	45·6	47·3	45·4	35·4	18·0	7·7	2·6
Italy										
Men	26·8	66·9	89·5	95·7	93·1	86·8	74·9	41·9	16·4	3·5
Women	21·2	42·6	33·1	27·7	26·1	23·3	13·0	7·3	2·8	0·7
UK										
Men	37·4	88·4	96·2	97·5	97·2	95·6	92·1	82·1	28·8	7·7
Women	33·9	60·2	44·5	49·2	61·5	58·6	49·1	28·5	11·1	2·6
1975										
W. Germany										
Men	37·0	76·7	89·0	97·5	97·4	94·0	87·0	62·4	17·2	6·3
Women	32·9	68·0	55·5	47·4	47·8	46·1	37·8	15·8	6·6	2·0
Italy										
Men	23·2	66·8	89·5	95·8	94·1	88·1	76·8	42·4	17·6	5·0
Women	17·8	42·8	37·4	30·0	28·7	24·4	16·3	7·4	3·2	0·8
UK										
Men	33·1	89·6	96·7	97·9	97·6	96·3	93·9	84·3	31·4	8·8
Women	29·1	65·8	50·0	56·8	67·0	64·7	53·4	30·4	11·1	2·4

Note: There are no figures for the UK for 1960 and 1968, as the UK was not then a member of the EEC.

Source: European Labour Force Sample Survey.

It appears that there is no way in which the data support the view that other entrants to the workforce are more sensitive to unemployment than young people are. The fact that female labour-force participation has continued to increase without any corresponding increase in the proportion of first-job seekers among the unemployed suggests that prime-age women entering the workforce have relatively little difficulty getting a job. This raises the possibility that employers may discriminate in favour of prime-age women entering the workforce, a possibility which is considered further in section 6.9.

It appears that in most essential respects the school-leaver hypothesis is correct, although on the specific issue of why school-leavers are more vulnerable than other first-job seekers its explanation is inadequate. It is true that school-leavers do not respond a great deal to the unemployment situation, but neither, it appears, do other entrants to the labour force.

6.8 SELECTIVE-REDUNDANCY HYPOTHESIS

The data provide only weak support for the selective-redundancy hypothesis. It is to be expected that redundancies will be most significant at the onset of recession. Redundancies were fairly common among young men aged twenty to twenty-four in West Germany and the UK in 1973; and by 1975, as the recession deepened, this tendency had to some extent reversed itself. Although consistent with the hypothesis, this is insufficient to confirm it.

It is difficult to find additional evidence either for or against the hypothesis. Little is known about the effects of redundancy payments, and even less about the extent of LIFO practices. Until more data are collected from individual firms, it will be impossible to assess the significance of selective redundancy.[14]

6.9 TREND HYPOTHESES

It is difficult to test the trend hypotheses, because of the lack of comparability in the data for different periods. Nevertheless, the predictions of the rival hypotheses diverge so much that, even allowing for the data limitations, some assessment can be made of their validity.

The first hypothesis asserts that increasing dissatisfaction with work is motivating a higher frequency of job-changing among young people. A comparison of workers' attitudes in the UK in 1971 and 1975 indicates a marginal increase in dissatisfaction with present employment; it is more pronounced among women than among men, although on the whole women still tend to be more satisfied with their work than are men.[15] However, this increasing dissatisfaction may simply represent the short-term deterioration in the employment situation, which has obliged workers to remain in unsatisfactory jobs because new work is difficult to find. The other prediction, that the frequency of job changing has increased, is not borne out. Whereas an early postwar study of Glasgow youth and a sample of school-leavers in 1954 suggest that young people were then changing jobs on average about once a year, more recent data for the UK suggest that under-eighteen-year-olds now change jobs about once in every two years. It appears, therefore, that an increased frequency of job-changing cannot explain the rising trend of youth unemployment.

The second hypothesis asserts that rising youth unemployment is a consequence of an increased supply of young workers and greater competition for jobs from women. The increasing supply of young workers has been very popular as an explanation of rising youth unemployment in the United States.[16] Unfortunately, the evidence suggests that it does not apply to the European experience of the 1970s. The postwar boom in births now affects the employment prospects of prime-age workers of twenty-five to thirty-four; in the 1970s the number of young people entering the workforce has declined (although an increase can be expected again in the next few years). On the other hand, the trend for the labour-force participation of married women to increase has continued, although with somewhat reduced momentum. This suggests that increasing competition for jobs may be damaging the employment prospects of young workers. If this has occurred, the duration of youth unemployment may be expected to have increased, and, indeed, this is what seems to have happened. For example, in the study of Glasgow youth referred to earlier, only 8 per cent of the young unemployed were out of work for more than six months, while the EEC statistics suggest that 20 per cent or more is now the norm (once again, though, it is difficult to distinguish the effect of cyclical changes in the rate of unemployment from the underlying long-term trend).

There is little evidence that displacement of young people by married women has been concentrated in particular industries. It is true that direct displacement of youths by women appears to have occurred in some activities, such as retailing; but, on the other hand, employment of women has also increased in banking and insurance, where it has been largely at the expense of adult men. The displacement appears to have pervaded the whole of industry. Recent evidence (see section 2.6) suggests that this may be owing to a worsening opinion of young people among employers.

Subject to the qualifications noted above, it appears that the evidence is in favour of the second hypothesis rather than the first. If dissatisfaction with work is increasing, it does not seem to be reflected in more frequent job-changing. On the other hand, increasing female labour-force participation is a continuing feature of most industralised economies, and this, coupled with the worsening 'image' of young workers, may explain the increasing duration of youth unemployment. But, until better data become available, this conclusion must remain a tentative one.

6.10   CONCLUSION

It has been established that two of the theories presented in Chapter 4 have a direct bearing on the youth-unemployment problem. The first is the job-search theory, which explains why young people are prone to unemployment even in periods of relative prosperity. The second is the school-leaver hypothesis, which explains the vulnerability of young people at times of recession.

A number of the other theories appear to be relevant, although for the time being their precise connection with unemployment must remain a matter of conjecture. The seasonal-unemployment hypothesis and the life-cycle unemployment hypothesis together explain well the industrial distribution of the youth labour force: they suggest that the youth-unemployment problem is very much tied up with the employment problems of particular industries. Of the trend hypotheses, the one concerned with increasing female participation performs best: it suggests that competition from women workers may account for the rising trend in youth unemployment.

7 Policy

7.1 INTRODUCTION

Most current debate on the alleviation of youth unemployment has focused on remedies for cyclical unemployment, and it therefore seems appropriate to begin by considering this aspect of policy. Two main types of measure have been advocated, concerned respectively with promoting the demand for labour and reducing its supply. These are considered in turn in sections 7.2 and 7.3. Section 7.4 examines the implications of this discussion for current UK policy. The next two sections consider the other aspects of youth unemployment: frictional unemployment owing to job-changing, and the increasing competition for jobs which is associated with the rising trend of unemployment. Section 7.7 makes proposals for a youth employment policy to be implemented at the industry level. The policy implications of the study are summarised in section 7.8.

7.2 JOB CREATION: STIMULATING THE DEMAND FOR LABOUR

When evaluating job-creation policies there are at least five key issues which must be resolved.

(1) Is it possible to increase employment among young workers without reducing employment among other groups? In other words, does job creation generate a net increase in employment, or does it merely redistribute jobs among different groups? In particular,
(2) will job creation increase taxation and so reduce output by impairing incentives, or
(3) will job creation worsen the balance of payments, and so make countervailing deflationary measures necessary?
(4) Should job-creation projects in the public sector be used to produce marketed output?

(5) To what extent is an employment subsidy preferable to direct job creation through public-sector projects?

These issues are considered in turn below.

(1) A short answer is that job-creation policies can increase aggregate employment; indeed, policies initially directed at one group of workers may indirectly increase employment among other groups of workers too. The main restriction is that the unemployment must be involuntary in the Keynesian sense (see section 3.4).

Consider, for example, a public-sector project employing 100 youths for a year. When unemployment is involuntary there will be no difficulty in recruiting youths at the prevailing money wage. Private-sector incomes will rise by 100 times the difference between the post-tax wage and the level of unemployment benefit. A proportion of this additional income will be spent on goods purchased from the private sector, and this will increase private-sector employment in all age groups. The increase in private-sector employment will further augment private incomes, and so lead to further spending, and further increases in employment. By the time this 'multiplier effect' has worked itself out, there will be more than 100 youths in employment (100 in the public sector and the rest in the private sector) and higher levels of employment in other age groups too.[1]

But suppose now that unemployment is voluntary. Young people will be willing to take up the newly created jobs in the public sector only if the money wage offered is above the prevailing level; otherwise they will prefer to remain without work. But, if the project offers employment at above the prevailing wage, workers who are already employed in the private sector will also be attracted, and private employers will have to match the higher money wages in order to retain employees. Their higher labour costs will lead to higher private-sector prices. So far as the newly employed workers are concerned, the higher prices nullify the effect of the higher money wage and leave them with the same standard of living as before. Once they realise that the real wage is no higher, they will quit, because at this wage they prefer to remain unemployed. A further increase in money wages will be necessary to maintain employment. But this in turn will lead to higher prices and so to an inflationary spiral. Without the inflation, none of the newly created jobs will be taken. With the inflation, expenditure on job creation must increase continuously just to keep the employment situation stable.[2]

(2) When considering whether job creation will increase taxation, it must of course be recognised that it is possible to finance public expenditure also by borrowing or by increasing the money supply. However, these policies merely shift the burden forward in time; their effect is to 'tax' wealth by respectively lowering bond prices and reducing the real value of the currency.

Consider the tax burden of a public-sector employment project producing non-marketed output. We assume throughout that unemployment is involuntary. The 'balanced-budget multiplier theorem' asserts that the increased value of output generated by the public expenditure will be just sufficient to meet the tax liability.[3] This means that private-sector output remains unchanged, and the increase in total output is equal to the increase in public expenditure.

It is clear that as a result of job creation a constant amount of private-sector output has to be shared among a larger number of employees, so that for each worker the private-sector component of real expenditure is reduced. On the other hand, public-sector output has increased proportionately more than aggregate output, so that the public-sector component of real expenditure is increased. This change in the composition of real expenditure is associated with higher tax rates, which may act as a disincentive to the supply of effort. This is because additional tax payments do not lead directly to the allocation of more public output to the individual taxpayer.[4] Even if they did, it is possible that the consumer's valuation of public output would be much lower than his valuation of private output of similar cost, so that higher taxes would still have a disincentive effect.

The disincentive effect on effort may reduce hours of work or encourage total withdrawal from the labour force, discourage workers from pursuing promotion or moving to higher-paid jobs, as well as discourage entrepreneurs from taking risks. However, if the unemployment is involuntary and affects all groups of workers, the disincentive effect on hours of work and labour-force participation is irrelevant, for workers are already supplying less labour than they wish to; the disincentive effect merely means that the shortfall in the amount of labour supplied is less than it would otherwise be. But the other disincentives may be sufficient to lead to a more rigid and less progressive economy.

(3) Concern over the balance of payments has probably deterred many countries from pursuing job creation more actively. Its effect on the balance of payments depends crucially on how it is financed. If it is financed out of current taxation, aggregate disposable income will remain unchanged and there will be no effect on trade flows *via* consumer spending (although, if the job-creation project uses materials which have an import content, there may be some effect on trade). But, if the job creation is financed by borrowing, aggregate disposable income will rise. Consumer spending on imports will increase, and the buoyant home market will encourage exporters to divert supplies to domestic consumers; imports will rise, exports fall, and the balance of trade deteriorate.

One way out of this dilemma is to arrange that the output of the job-creation programme is either an export, an import substitute, or an intermediate good used in the production of exports or import substitutes. In this way the direct effect of the output on trade may neutralise the indirect effect *via* consumer incomes. All of this suggests that, when evaluating a job-creation programme, both the method of financing it, and the type of output produced, are of paramount importance.

(4) The preceding discussion leads naturally to the question of whether the output of public-sector employment projects should be marketed. It certainly seems that in many cases the appropriate output will be a marketable good. It can be argued that normally marketing will be the most efficient way of rationing the distribution of the good; moreover, the 'price signals' generated by marketing will provide an indication of the utility of the good to consumers.

The arguments against marketed output are twofold.

The first argument is that marketing the output would damage employment in the private sector of the economy. There would certainly be individual cases of redundancy in firms producing competing goods. However, there would be no reduction in aggregate private-sector employment, even where public sector output is financed out of current taxation. If the public-sector project breaks even, the value of the additional factor income generated by the public sector is exactly equal to the value of the additional output sold, so that the net impact on the private sector is zero. If the public sector makes a profit, taxes can be reduced by the same amount and so discretionary expenditure on private-sector output can increase to compensate exactly for the earlier diversion of expenditure to the public sector. If the public sector makes a loss, the effect is much the same as if the output had not been marketed at all. In all cases the result is the same: private-sector employment remains unchanged, and public-sector employment increases by the number of workers employed on the project.

The second argument is that specific public-sector projects servicing local markets would compete unfairly with established private enterprises, in the sense that the public project could sustain losses which a small local competitor could not. If the public projects were only temporary, the closing down and subsequent reopening of small businesses would be associated with considerable dislocation of production. Thus public intervention in supply would increase business risks in the private sector and so raise the required rate of profit and deter investment. This argument would not have the same force, however, if exports or import substitutes were produced, for here the effects could be felt only in the much wider world market, which would be better able to absorb the 'shocks' of public intervention in supply.

(5) The final issue concerns the respective merits of public-sector projects and employment subsidies. This is a complex issue involving many theoretical and practical considerations.

Selective employment subsidies are difficult to administer. A subsidy confined to young workers would tend to displace large numbers of unskilled older workers. Checking that firms who claimed the subsidy had not made other workers redundant would be difficult, particularly in industries employing part-time and casual labour, and in non-unionised industries, where no independent source of information is available.

A subsidy on all young workers would normally have to be paid not only on those workers recruited in response to the subsidy, but also on all the other young workers who would have been recruited anyway. The induced recruitment will normally be only a small proportion of total recruitment; the proportion will be large only if the subsidy is high relative to the average wage and the elasticity of the demand for labour is also high.[5] Thus, the cost to the exchequer of each additional job created is considerably in excess of the subsidy on the incremental worker. It would be difficult to discriminate between the incremental workers and the rest. One way would be to pay subsidies to firms for an increase in the total number of young workers employed over a period, with deductions for any decrease in the numbers of other workers. But the administrative costs would be high, and the scheme would be subject to abuse – for example, by firms closing down and starting up again under a new name.

It appears, therefore, that the best kind of employment subsidy is probably the simplest: namely, a fixed percentage subsidy on all employed workers, irrespective of age. Such a subsidy could be administered through the national insurance scheme by adjusting employers' contributions. It would have few displacement effects, since wage relativities would remain unchanged. It would be impartial in its effect on individual firms within the country, but would make exporting and import-substituting firms more competitive relative to their foreign rivals. It would create additional jobs, which would favour young people to the extent that they predominate among the involuntarily unemployed. Unlike public-sector employment projects, the scheme would generate output known to be relevant to consumer wants, and would provide jobs with a potential for long-term employment. The main disadvantage would be the very high tax cost. However, if the tax were borne by people supplying the types of labour which were in excess supply, the disincentive effect of the tax would be of no consequence. A few more people voluntarily unemployed would simply mean more vacancies for the involuntarily unemployed to step into. The net effect of the measure would be to reduce the real wage of those whose labour is in excess supply, and thereby increase aggregate employment. Union response to the measure would depend upon how clearly they recognised the tax implications. The response of other trading nations would depend upon how clearly they recognised the balance-of-payments effects of the subsidy.

It appears that an employment subsidy is essentially an 'all or nothing' measure. It is difficult, and quite possibly undesirable, to make it a selective measure. On a theoretical level it has many features which make it preferable to public-sector employment projects. But its fiscal implications mean that it would require a very strong political will to carry through the policy to its logical conclusion.

7.3   REDUCING THE SUPPLY OF LABOUR

The supply of labour can be reduced in a number of ways.

The most direct method is to encourage young people to continue their education, either at school or at a training centre. The continuation can be made compulsory, or can be achieved through financial incentive; experience suggests that simply making the facilities available is not enough.[6]

Any continuation policy must recognise that in a period of recession the main candidates for continuation are in the lower ranges of ability, and the provision of conventional further education would be fruitless. More appropriate are remedial teaching of the 'three Rs', or vocational training, or some mixture of the two. However, the vocational training has to be fairly general, since, despite recent advances in manpower planning, it is difficult to predict the future skill requirements of industry, particularly during the period of uncertainty which is characteristic of a recession. An advantage of vocational training is that it may provide motivation for remedial academic study, as well as introduce young people to the disciplines of working life.

The main difficulty with organising continuation of education on a countercyclical basis lies in establishing a proper syllabus and maintaining teaching standards when there is no continuity in the programme. It would be very expensive to maintain a permanent staff to service an intermittent demand, but equally it is difficult to maintain standards if teachers and instructors are recruited as temporary workers and have no time to co-ordinate their work. Moreover, much of the benefit of these courses is likely to be lost if, at the end, the young people return to being unemployed.

The other ways of reducing the supply of labour are essentially methods for redistributing the burden of unemployment, since they involve withdrawing people from the labour force but giving them nothing else to do. They include early retirement, short-time working (sometimes called 'work-sharing'), retirement of part-time or married women workers, and so forth. The idea is that the withdrawal of these workers creates vacancies for young people to take up. It is usual to provide these workers with incentives so that their withdrawal is voluntary, but this imposes an additional financial burden on the state. Instead of providing relatively low benefits to unemployed young workers, it is necessary to pay higher benefits to inactive older workers. If the additional benefits are financed by borrowing then consumer incomes will increase and the balance of payments will deteriorate as a result of a higher demand for inputs. On the other hand, if the benefits are financed by taxation, then, unless the incidence of the taxation is carefully controlled, there may be disincentive effects which lead employers to reduce the demand for labour.

Unlike job creation, policies for reducing the supply of labour cannot resolve the basic problem of unemployment. They can only make the situation more palatable, either by keeping young people occupied on improvised remedial or vocational courses, or by shifting the burden of unemployment onto those better qualified – economically or socially – to bear it.

7.4 AN APPRAISAL OF COUNTERCYCLICAL POLICIES IN THE UK

The UK government was one of the first to respond to the general rise in unemployment which affected many countries in 1974–5. It has experimented with a variety of policies. The demand for labour has been promoted by public-sector employment projects and by selective employment subsidies. Attempts have been made to reduce the supply of labour by recruiting the young unemployed onto training programmes, and by encouraging the early retirement of selected groups of workers. Although it can be criticised for failing to draw on experience with similiar policies in the prewar period, the government's eclectic approach has been fairly successful, and this is reflected in the increasing amount of public funds being devoted to youth employment policy.[7]

The implementation of policy has been mainly in the hands of the Manpower Services Commission, which has adopted the enlightened practice of regularly reviewing the impact of its measures, and publishing its conclusions. The following paragraphs review UK experience, and consider what lessons can be drawn for future policy.

In October 1975 a Job Creation Programme (JCP) was established to provide temporary jobs of 'social value'. Workers were paid the union-negotiated wage for the job (where applicable). In view of the unskilled nature of the work, this meant that many workers took a drop in income to work on JCP (in 1976 a sample of workers received a median wage of £26 per week under the JCP, compared with £27 in their previous job and £29 in their subsequent job).[8] The gross cost to the Exchequer was £2300 per man year, but, after allowance for savings of unemployment and supplementary benefit and the gain in tax and insurance contributions, the net cost was about 45 per cent of this. Taking into account the cost of travel to work, it appears that in some cases the financial gain to the unemployed worker from joining the JCP was fairly marginal; even so, most of the projects sponsored under the scheme were well subscribed (on average about 80 per cent of places were filled).

A Recruitment Subsidy for School-Leavers (RSSL), organised by the Department of Employment, was introduced at the same time as the JCP. It offered employers £5 per week for six months for recruiting a school-leaver who had been unemployed since the summer. A sample survey of firms who claimed the subsidy revealed that only 24 per cent believed that it had influenced the number of school-leavers they had recruited, while 14 per cent claimed they had reduced recruitment of other groups as a result; the groups that suffered appear to have been adult females and part-time workers such as students.[9] It appears that the subsidy led to a net increase in recruitment in only about 10 per cent of the firms sampled.

The way the RSSL was administered created an incentive for employers to discriminate in favour of school-leavers eligible for the RSSL. Yet 66 per cent of firms recruiting five or more RSSL school-leavers and 29 per cent of firms recruiting one to four RSSL school-leavers also recruited school-leavers for whom no subsidy was claimed. And throughout the period of the subsidy there were many unemployed school-leavers eligible for the RSSL for whom no jobs could be found. This suggests either that many of the unemployed school-leavers have attributes which make them virtually 'unemployable', or that long-term unemployment is regarded by some employers as itself a sign of 'unemployability'.

The high cost of a general recruitment subsidy, coupled with the ineffectiveness of the subsidy in dealing with certain categories of the unemployed, suggested to the government that in future recruitment subsidies should be concentrated on the most disadvantaged groups. As a result, in October 1976 a Youth Employment Subsidy (YES) was introduced, paying £10 per week for every recruit who had been unemployed for six months or more. Unlike the RSSL, the YES was available for all young people under twenty, whether they had recently left school or not.

A sample survey of firms claiming the subsidy suggests that it was no more successful than the RSSL in increasing net employment.[10] Furthermore, the way the subsidy was administered created a strong incentive for employers to substitute the long-term unemployed for the short-term unemployed. If it is true that on average the long-term unemployed are less able workers than the short-term unemployed, the initial effect of the subsidy would have been to encourage employers to employ less able in preference to more able workers. However, after the scheme had been in operation for some time the long-term unemployed would have contained many of the discriminated-against more able workers. When these became eligible under the scheme, employers would probably have preferred them to the less able workers. Thus in the long run the scheme would have had only limited success in improving the prospects of less able workers. This 'success' would have been achieved largely by increasing the duration of unemployment among more able workers. While some people would commend the equalisation of the duration of unemployment on grounds of equity, it must be recognised that it has probably been achieved at the expense of efficiency, since it involves the substitution of less able for more able labour.

In September 1976 a Work Experience Programme (WEP) was introduced, to provide unemployed sixteen- to eighteen-year-olds with a first-hand experience of working life. A scheme is approved only if it will not disrupt the employer's normal recruitment and training programmes, and if the co-operation of local trades unions and employees is obtained. About 18,000 trainees per annum receive an allowance of £19.50 per week, free of tax and insurance contributions; the employers receive nothing. Unlike the JCP, which was dominated by male workers, the WEP has been taken up mainly by women.[11] This is partly because women were often unsuited to the heavy manual work involved on the JCP, and partly because the WEP has been concentrated in distribution, where the female labour force is large.

It appears that the WEP has not been very successful as far as the young people themselves are concerned. Relatively few WEP schemes have been fully subscribed and, as with the JCP, about half of the people on them leave early. It is therefore somewhat surprising that the WEP has been continued, as one of the main elements in the current Youth Opportunities Programme (see below). Perhaps the attraction to the government is that detailed administration of the scheme is delegated to the sponsoring firms.

Besides the major schemes described above there have been a number of smaller projects directed at minority groups. These include a Job Introduction Scheme for disabled workers, and a long-standing Community Industry Scheme for chronic job-changers and others who cannot settle into working life.

Young people have also benefited from other, more general schemes, such as the Temporary Employment Subsidy for workers liable to be made redundant (about 23 per cent of subsidised workers were estimated to be under twenty-five). There has also been a Job Release Scheme enabling workers within one year of statutory retirement age to claim a weekly tax-free allowance if they give up their job or refrain from claiming unemployment benefit. To begin with, most of those taking advantage of the scheme had already been made redundant, and were probably not actively seeking work but, subsequently, unemployed workers were made ineligible for release.

The present employment policy was implemented in April 1978. There are two main programmes, the Youth Opportunites Programme (YOP) and the Special Temporary Employment Programme (STEP). The YOP pays young people of between sixteen and eighteen an allowance of £19·50 per week, free of tax and national insurance. The main elements of the programme are

(1) assessment or employment-induction courses lasting about two weeks, to help the young person assess the type of work he prefers;

(2) short industrial courses to introduce young people to a specific occupation as a basis for future employment as a semi-skilled operative (also remedial courses);

(3) work experience on employers' premises, continuing the role of the WEP (also project-based work experience);

(4) training workshops, providing experience in a variety of skills for those not likely to be attracted by a formal course (although goods and services are produced, this is only incidental to the main purpose of the programme); and

(5) community service, to allow young people to exercise responsibility, and so perhaps motivate further education or formal vocational training.

The philosophy underlying the YOP is to offer low-level training rather than unskilled temporary work to the young unemployed. Although not strictly a continuation of education, it is nevertheless a means of reducing the supply of labour rather than stimulating the demand. It provides on-the-job training, but without the job. In view of the fact that no output is produced, the allowances offered to trainees seem rather generous. It must be recognised that the injection of government funds, estimated at £160 million per annum gross, or £80 million net of savings in state benefits, will have a multiplier effect on incomes elsewhere in the economy. Unless taxes are raised, total incomes may increase by £100 million or so, and this may lead to additional imports of £30 million or more, without any stimulus to exports. If the allowances were cut to the level of supplementary benefit, the young people would still gain to the extent of the value of the training they receive, while the balance-of-payments cost of the programme would be virtually eliminated. So long as they remain at their present level, there is the risk that the government may have to implement deflationary measures to neutralise the balance-of-payments effects of the YOP, resulting in the loss of jobs elsewhere. If this occurs, the creation of training places under the YOP will have been at least partly offset by job losses among other groups of workers.

The second programme, STEP, is designed to provide temporary jobs for up to 25,000 people per annum on schemes of benefit to the community. It is founded on a broadly similar basis to the JCP, which it replaces. Preference is given to the provision of jobs for people aged nineteen to twenty-four who have been continuously unemployed for more than six months and people over twenty-five who have not had a job for at least twelve months.

The main criticism of the STEP is that it is oriented towards producing the wrong sort of output. As with the JCP before it, explicitly profit-making projects are excluded. Although the work that is done – for example, in assisting old people – meets a real need, it can be argued that that need would be better met by more qualified helpers. If the young people were employed instead on producing marketed output – in particular, exports or import substitutes – the improvement in the balance of payments would permit the government to increase expenditure on social services, and so recruit professional workers.

There are a variety of projects which could be undertaken, from renovating monuments which would attract foreign tourists, and improving roads and terminal facilities at ports, to farming land awaiting redevelopment in urban areas, and increasing the frequency of postal collections and deliveries in the commercial areas of major towns. It would be advantageous if such projects were organised with teams of youngsters as paid sub-contractors. This would give young people some idea of the commercial criteria which govern employment in industry, and help them to appreciate the standard of service which paying customers expect.

To summarise the UK experience, it appears that

(1) the diagnosis of youth unemployment as involuntary is basically correct: there is no difficulty in recruiting young workers at the prevailing wage onto job-creation programmes;

(2) the attempt to devise selective subsidies to create additional jobs has largely failed: the main effect has been to redistribute the burden of unemployment, though, even with a subsidy, employers are cau-

tious about substituting the long-term unemployed for other groups of workers;

(3) there has been considerable emphasis on reducing the supply of labour by encouraging the unemployed to take up work experience, but, on the other hand, there has been little attempt to organise remedial education: only time will tell whether the relative neglect of basic literacy and numeracy among the young unemployed has been the right policy; and

(4) there has been too little consideration of the fiscal and balance of payments implications of the schemes: job creation is preferable to work experience in that, at the very least, some output is produced, but the importance of this distinction does not seem to have been appreciated, nor has the potential for making constructive use of the output been realised.

7.5 MINIMISING FRICTIONAL UNEMPLOYMENT

Frictional unemployment owing to frequent job-changing by young people has been a perennial problem. If the frequency of job-changing is simply imputed to the 'immaturity' of youth, a possible remedy is to raise the school-leaving age. This delays entry into the labour force until attitudes to work have matured. It seems quite likely that, in the past, raising the school-leaving age from twelve to fourteen, and then to fifteen, led to some improvement. But experience with subsequent raising of the age to sixteen suggests that 'diminishing returns' soon set in. The longer young people of low ability remain at school, the more difficulty there is in motivating their studies, and the more difficulty they may experience later in adapting to the discipline and routine of working life. In any case, to the extent that job-changing represents a process of search, it will accompany entry into working life at whatever age it occurs, so that raising the school-leaving age merely delays the process rather than avoids it altogether.

Job-changing *per se* is not the whole of the frictional unemployment problem: it leads to unemployment only because of the gap in time between leaving one job and starting the next. An alternative approach to frictional unemployment is to take the need for job-changing as a datum, and to attempt to reduce the duration of unemployment between jobs.

A number of writers have suggested that compulsory notification to the public employment service of all vacancies, hirings and separations concerning young people would materially assist in this. It would help the employment service to take the initiative in approaching the newly unemployed with information about vacancies. It would enable an early diagnosis of potentially chronic job-changing, and also isolate those employers whose turnover of young people is particularly high. This in turn would make it possible to organise special employment projects for chronic job-changers and to take appropriate action against known bad employers, even if this only involved warning job-seekers about them. Although operation of the system could be quite expensive, it would enable policy to be focused on the relatively small 'hard core' of individuals and firms who are involved in a large proportion of all separations.

Some writers have gone so far as to suggest compulsory placement through the public employment service.[12] This seems to have little to commend it. Informal contacts are a very convenient way of finding a job, and workers placed in this way often stay longer with their employers than do those placed through official agencies. The costs of increased bureaucracy would almost certainly outweigh any advantages to workers or employers that might stem from a nominally wider of choice of jobs or applicants through official channels.

An important factor in frictional unemployment, and one that has received little attention from policy-makers, is that many separations occur at very short notice. This means that the employer often has difficulty in maintaining continuity of production, if he cannot immediately hire a replacement, while the worker does not have time to arrange another job to go to and so becomes unemployed. Separations at short notice often occur as the result of personal dispute, following which the employee quits or is dismissed for disciplinary reasons. If a period of notice were required from both sides prior to the separation, the employer could have time to recruit a replacement and the worker could have more time to find another job. If, in addition, a grievance procedure were followed, involving an external conciliator or arbitrator, it is possible that during the period of notice the two sides might be able to resolve their diffferences. Certainly the grievance procedure would help to alleviate the mutual distrust of employer and employee while the period of notice was being worked out. If successful, this arrangement would reduce both the frequency of job-changing – because conciliation would allow a better understanding between employer and employee – and also the duration of unemployment, since the worker could have time to look for a job before he becomes unemployed.

The arrangement would also integrate well with the proposal, discussed earlier, for compulsory notification of separations. The intention to separate would be notified to the employment service and if a young person were involved they would send a conciliator to establish the reason for the separation. It is possible that the reason would be quite straightforward: dissatisfaction with the type of work, or a desire for a spell of leave, or the employer's need to cut back his labour force. In other cases the situation might be more difficult (and acrimonious), and it is here that conciliation would be potentially most effective. At the same time as conciliation was proceeding, contingency plans would be made on behalf of both employer and employee. The young worker would be sent a list of vacancies (ideally, chosen in the light of the preferences revealed by the reasons for the separation). Interviews would be set up with potential employers selected by the worker. Because of their close involvement with the young worker in his previous job changes, the employment service would be in a good position to provide a reference for the young worker (at his request). The provisional vacancy created by the separation would be notified to other young workers, and the employer would be able to see what calibre of applicants he could attract as a replacement. In the light of all this evidence, employer and employee could reach a final decision on whether or not to separate.

7.6 REVERSING THE TREND

There are several reasons why the rising trend of youth unemployment seems likely to continue.

First, the number of school-leavers available for employment will increase over the next few years. Although the numbers reaching retiring age will increase too, there will be a substantial gap between the numbers entering and the numbers leaving the workforce (see Table 7.1).

Secondly, a recent survey of sixteen countries indicates that the trend for women's share of employment to increase shows no sign of abating.[13] This suggests not only that female labour-force participation holds up well at the onset of a recession, but also that in some respects women are now in a better competitive position than men.

Thirdly, it seems reasonable to predict that over the next decade opportunities for unskilled work in developed countries are likely to contract. The increasing supply of unskilled industrial labour in

TABLE 7.1   Projected changes in the labour force: UK 1978–82

Mid-year to mid-year	Numbers (thousands)		
	School-leavers available for employment	Those reaching normal retiring age	Projected increase
1977–8	683	349	193
1978–9	691	353	176
1979–80	707	415	159
1980–1	707	383	153
1981–2	705	364	242

Source: Department of Employment Gazette, 86 (1978) 326. Reproduced by permission of the Controller of HMSO.

Note: The numbers in the right-hand column do not represent the difference between the other two columns, because changes in labour-force participation have been allowed for.

developing countries is likely to create severe world competition in the supply of labour-intensive goods. This has already occured in textiles, and is now leading to the 'export of jobs' in the assembly of certain consumer durables. Automation is likely to have a considerable impact on the service sector: in particular, computerisation at point of sale may well lead to job losses in retailing, where a large proportion of young people are employed. However, these losses may be offset to some extent by gains elsewhere in the service sector, owing, for example, to the continued growth of international tourism.

On balance, there is likely to be a deficiency of jobs suitable for young people. The industries which are the traditional employers of young people have only limited prospects for creating additional jobs (and in any case such jobs would not be desirable if long-term career prospects were poor). This suggests that more jobs must be found for young people in industries which at present employ few of them. In certain industries there may be scope for reducing age limits on recruitment, although in some cases (for instance, chemicals and transport) safety considerations may preclude the employment of very young workers. It is of course quite possible that in the long run market forces will solve the problem by reducing the wages of unskilled workers relative to skilled workers, and so encourage the creation of more unskilled jobs. But this process depends on employers' investing in the development of new production techniques which downgrade the skill requirements of labour. This may be a lengthy process, and one which it is too expensive for any one employer to embark on alone. Thus, there is a case for a concerted effort to investigate the possibility of substituting young unskilled workers for older skilled workers in industries where at present young people are not normally employed.

7.7 AN INDUSTRIAL POLICY FOR YOUTH EMPLOYMENT

It has been demonstrated in this book that the early careers of young workers are to a large extent determined by the employment practices of a few 'key' industries, such as distribution, construction and textiles. These industries recruit large numbers of young workers straight from school, and retain them until they leave as young adults to seek higher-paid work.

By and large, such industries offer very poor on-the-job training. To some extent this may reflect the skill-potential of the workers they recruit, and also their high labour turnover, which makes it uneconomic for the employer to invest in 'human capital'. But equally it could be argued that it is the poor quality of training which is responsible for the apparently low calibre of the employees and for the high turnover of labour.

One way out of this vicious circle is to pay firms for the training they provide. The employee could be asked to pay by deductions from his wage, or the state could subsidise the training. If a fairly general training in business methods were provided in a number of small modules (of, say, two to three months' duration), the training would not be unduly disrupted by an occasional change of employer. If the training were standardised at the industry level, workers could move freely between firms within the industry. However, it might be necessary to constrain job-changing to the extent that workers more than halfway through a module would be obliged to complete it before changing employer.

Employers would be paid for the training according to the results their employees achieved in a general examination, set by the Industry Training Board, on each module. Payment by results is essential, because it is well known that the examination success of trainees varies considerably from firm to firm, with small firms – which predominate in youth-intensive industries – doing worst.[14]

By making the incentive to train independent of the turnover rate, the scheme would encourage firms to devote more resources to training. The resulting improvement in the quality of training might well enchance job satisfaction among employees, and so reduce turnover.

There are other policies which could also be implemented at the industry level. We have already mentioned the need to increase the number of unskilled jobs for young people in industries where at present they are underrepresented. Such vacancies would be designed for young trainees, who would later graduate to more responsible jobs in the industry.

We have also referred to the need for more enlightened personnel policies, and for organised grievance procedures. Day-to-day administration of such procedures is best organised by area rather than by industry, with each administrator handling all employers in a local labour market. But general aspects of policy are best formulated at the industry level, since they are closely connected with the operating methods specific to the industry.

Finally, there is the problem of the cyclical sensitivity of certain industries: for example, during the current recession a relatively high proportion of unemployed youths were made redundant from the construction industry. If the government intends to sponsor counter-cyclical job-creation programmes, it seems reasonable that the initiative for such programmes should originate at the industry level. A list of low-priority projects could be established during periods of prosperity, so that a work programme could be allocated to young people without delay at the onset of recession.

All of this suggests that the scope of the Industry Training Boards' activities should be considerably widened. They should be encouraged to extend existing arrangements for rewarding employers' contributions to on-the-job training, to investigate ways of developing new job openings for young people, to develop codes of conduct regarding the hiring and firing of young employees, and to plan countercyclical job-creation programmes. Trade unions can probably be relied upon to uphold the interests of older workers. The onus is on organisations such as the Training Boards to promote the interests of young workers at the industry level.

7.8 SUMMARY AND CONCLUSION

One of the main aims of this book has been to establish that the youth-unemployment problem is not just the result of the current recession. It is true that the length and severity of the recession has been a major factor exacerbating the situation, particularly where unemployment among school-leavers is concerned. But it cannot be assumed that if and when the recovery comes the problem will simply disappear. It is almost certain that frictional unemployment owing to job-changing will remain a serious problem, and that on top of this an increasing shortage of jobs for unskilled young workers is likely to emerge. Although market forces, acting through the wage rate, may alleviate the latter problem, the process is likely to be a slow one, and one that will meet resistance on both social and political grounds.

If youth unemployment will not go away, it seems only sensible to develop policies now which not merely create temporary jobs, or delay entry into working life, but offer young people systematic career development leading to stable skilled employment in their early twenties (if not before). Such policies are certainly feasible, and on economic grounds are as much to the advantage to the rest of society as they are to the young people themselves.

Appendix: The EEC Labour Force Sample Survey

The Labour Force Sample Survey is conducted biennially in the spring by the member states of the Community, in accordance with regulation (EEC) 2723/72 of the Council of Ministers, dated 19 December 1972.

The sampling and the visits to the households are carried out by the national statistical institutes, which are also responsible for coding the results. The Statistical Office of the European Communities is responsible for processing the data.

The survey covers all people whose normal or actual place of residence is in one of the member states of the Community during the week in question. In some countries it is not possible to include residents of collective households such as schools, hospitals and workers' hostels, but as the members of private households make up about 97 per cent of the total population of the Community the results may be regarded as generally reliable. The number of households sampled in West Germany, Italy and U.K. is between 60,000 and 100,000.

The information collected by the survey includes (a) the individual characteristics of all the persons in the households questioned; (b) the occupations of these persons (status, type of activity, hours of work, and so on) at the time of the survey and one year prior to it; and (c) the search for work, taking into account the type of employment sought, reasons for seeking it, and the length of time spent seeking it.

The main definitions used by the survey are as follows:

(1) *Members of private households.* Included in this group are those whose normal or actual place of residence is in one of the Community countries participating in the survey during the week in question, and who belong to a private household as defined in that country. People not considered to be members of a household are (a) people living in collective households, whether or not these have been included wholly or partially in the national sample survey, (b) people who have their legal residence in one of the member states

but usually live in another Community country or in a third country; and (c) national servicemen, even if they are living as members of a private household at the time of the survey.

(2) *People in employment.* People employed include all people of fourteen years and over who (a) have carried out paid work as their main occupation during the week in question; (b) are normally employed but during the week in question were not at work, because of illness, accident, holiday, strike or other circumstances; (c) have not worked for technical reasons or owing to bad weather; or (d) are carrying out unpaid work assisting in a family business or farm for more than 14 hours per week.

(3) *People who are unemployed.* Those people who have declared themselves to be unemployed are all those who come into one of the following categories: (a) employable workers who were unemployed and seeking paid work during the week in question because their employment contract had come to an end or had been temporarily suspended; (b) people who had had no previous employment or whose last professional status was not that of wage-earner (former employers, for instance) or who had not worked for a certain length of time and who were capable of working during the period in question and were seeking paid employment; (c) unemployed people capable of working immediately who had taken the necessary steps to start a new paid job but at a date subsequent to the date in question; and (d) people laid off temporarily or for an indefinite period without pay.

(4) *People seeking employment.* All those who stated that they were seeking paid employment at the time of the survey come into this category, which covers (a) employed people seeking another job; (b) people declared to be unemployed who have previously had work; (c) people who have declared themselves to be unemployed and are seeking work for the first time; and (d) people outside the working population at the time of the survey who are nevertheless seeking employment (for instance, pupils and students looking for work for the first time).

For further details see Eurostat, *Social Statistics*, no. 1, 1975, pp. 207–10, and *Labour Force Sample Survey* (Luxembourg, 1976) pp. 193–7.

Notes

CHAPTER 1

1. For a comparison of official measures of unemployment in different
   countries, see 'International Unemployment Statistics', *Department of
   Employment Gazette*, 84 (1976) 710–15. This paper takes as a norm the
   recommendations of the Eighth International Conference of Labour
   Statisticians organised by the International Labour Office (ILO). The
   principal discrepancies noted are that (a) all three countries – West
   Germany, Italy and the UK – exclude the temporarily sick and those
   temporarily suspended from work; (b) the UK excludes adult students
   seeking work; and (c) the UK and Italy include those who are not actively
   seeking work. For a consideration of the biases brought about through
   exclusion of the unregistered unemployed, see *Unemployment Statistics:
   Report of an Interdepartmental Working Party* (London: Her Majesty's
   Stationery Office, 1972); A. R. Thatcher, 'Statistics of Unemployment in the
   United Kingdom', *Department of Employment Gazette*, 82 (1974) 379–83, a
   revised version of which is contained in G. D. N. Worswick (ed.), *The
   Concept and Measurement of Involuntary Unemployment* (London: Allen &
   Unwin, 1976) pp. 83–94; and 'The Unregistered Unemployed in Great
   Britain', *Department of Employment Gazette*, 84, (1976) 1331–6. For a
   survey of the characteristics of the unregistered unemployed, see Office of
   Population Censuses and Surveys, *General Household Survey 1975* (London: HMSO, 1977), Table 5.18. The measurement of unemployment by the
   Statistical Office of the European Communities is described in D. Harris,
   'Assessment of Unemployment in the EEC', in Worswick (ed.), *op. cit.*, pp.
   95–106. In emphasing the limitations of official statistics, we are not
   endorsing some of the recent attempts to remeasure unemployment – for
   instance, J. B. Wood's *How Little Unemployment?* (London: Institute of
   Economic Affairs, 1975).
2. The social consequences of unemployment are considered in H. L. Beales
   and R. S. Lambert (eds), *Memoirs of the Unemployed* (London: Gollancz,
   1934); M. J. Hill *et al.*, *Men out of Work* (Cambridge: Cambridge University
   Press, 1973); D. Marsden and E. Duff, *Workless – Some Unemployed Men
   and Their Families* (Harmondsworth: Penguin, 1975); and, most recently,
   R. Harrison, 'The Demoralising Experience of Prolonged Unemployment',
   Department of Employment Gazette, 84 (1976) 339–48. The special problems of youth receive attention in A. E. Morgan, *The Needs of Youth*
   (London: King George's Jubilee Trust, 1939); and C. Cameron, A. Lush
   and G. Meara, *Disinherited Youth: A Report on the 18 + Age Group*

Enquiry Prepared for the Trustees of the Carnegie United Kingdom Trust (Edinburgh: T. & A. Constable, 1943).
3. For a statistical survey of recent trends in youth unemployment in the UK, see S. Mukherjee, *There's Work To Be Done: Unemployment and Manpower Policies* (London: Manpower Services Commission, 1974); and B. Showler, 'Youth Unemployment in Britain', paper presented to the Conference on Youth Unemployment in Great Britain and the Federal Republic of Germany, London, Nov 1976.
4. The cyclical sensitivity of youth unemployment in the UK has been examined in more detail by D. J. Smyth and P. D. Lowe, in 'The Vestibule to the Occupational Ladder and Unemployment: Some Econometric Evidence on United Kingdom Structural Unemployment', *Industrial and Labor Relations Review*, 23 (1970) 561–5. Young people are not alone in being vulnerable to unemployment in a recession; the same tends to be true of coloured Commonwealth immigrants and also of disabled workers.

CHAPTER 2

1. It is apparent that some of the studies reviewed in this chapter do not meet the standard of objectivity expected of modern social and economic surveys. In some cases it seems that the investigator's value judgements may have influenced his interpretation of the evidence, particularly where the evidence is essentially qualitative. Nevertheless, these interpretations are of interest, first for the light they shed on attitudes at the time, and secondly because they constitute hypotheses which may provide a framework for researchers designing new inquiries. These interpretations are therefore reported in the text, even though some of them may appear to the modern reader to be rather sweeping generalisations.
2. For a bibliography of the boy-labour problem see A. Freeman, *Boy Life and Labour: The Manufacture of Inefficiency* (London: P. S. King and Son, 1914). The major books and pamphlets are R. A. Bray, *Boy Labour and Apprenticeship* (London: Constable, 1911); S. J. Gibb, *Boy Labour and Unemployment*, 2nd ed. (London: Mowbray, 1910); A. Greenwood, *Juvenile Labour Exchanges and After Care* (London: P. S. King and Son, 1911); C. Jackson, *Unemployment and the Trade Unions* (London: Longman, 1910), Ch. 6; F. H. Keeling, *The Labour Exchange in Relation to Boy and Girl Labour* (London: P. S. King & Son, 1910); G. W. Knowles, *Juvenile Labour Exchanges* (Manchester: Sherratt, 1910); T. Percival, *Poor Law Children: Part 2* (London: Shaw & Sons, 1912). The most important articles are R. A. Bray, 'The Apprenticeship Question', *Economic Journal*, 19 (1909) 400–9; A. Greenwood, 'Blind Alley Labour', *Economic Journal*, 22 (1912) 309–14; A. Greenwood and J. E. Kettlewell, 'Some Statistics of Juvenile Employment and Unemployment', *Journal of the Royal Statistical Society*, 75 (1912) 744–53; C. Jackson, 'Apprenticeship and the Training of the Workman', *Edinburgh Review*, 216 (1912) 411–27; T. Jones, 'Unemployment, Boy Labour, and Continued Education, *Socialist Review*, 2 (1909) 857–70; and R. H. Tawney, 'Economics of Boy Labour', *Economic Journal*, 19 (1909) 517–37.

The antecedents of the boy-labour problem are traced in J. Gollan, *Youth in British Industry* (London: Gollancz, 1937), and Tawney, *op. cit.* The connection between the conditions of entry into working life and subsequent experience of unemployment was urged by several witnessess before the Labour Commission of 1894, and was given considerable emphasis in the Report of the Royal Commission on the Depression of Trade in 1886. Since the beginning of the nineteenth century, trade unionists had complained about the 'overstocking of trade with boys', and centuries earlier similar arguments were used when the statutes for the regulation of apprentices were introduced. However, the solution of the boy-labour problem did not become an integral part of employment policy as a whole until the reports of the Royal Commission on the Poor Laws and the Relief of Distress in 1909.

3. From W. H. Beveridge, *Unemployment: A Problem of Industry* (London: Longman, 1909) pp. 125–6.

4. Tawney, *op. cit.* For an earlier analysis of the age distribution of the workforce in various trades, see C. Booth (ed.), *Life and Labour of the People in London*, vol. IX: *Comparisons, Survey and Conclusions* (London: Macmillan, 1897) pp. 43–52. For a follow-up study, see A. L. Bowley, 'London Occupations and Industries', in H. Llewellyn Smith (ed.), *The New Survey of London Life and Labour*, vol. I: *Forty Years of Change* (London: P. S. King & Son, 1930) pp. 315–40.

5. Suppose that the working life of the individual is fourteen to sixty-four inclusive. If the workforce consists of one person of every age, there will be seven people in the fourteen to twenty age group ('boys') and forty-four in the twenty-one to sixty-four age group ('men'). Hence the ratio of men to boys will be approximately six to one. If this ratio is reduced, then, on average, the number of men retiring each year will be less than the number of boys coming of age; and so, unless the workforce as a whole expands, some boys will have to become redundant on their twenty-first birthday.

6. An inquiry conducted by Tawney in Glasgow in 1907 compared the careers of two groups of sixteen- to twenty-one-year-olds, the first consisting of 100 tradesmen, the second of 150 unskilled workers ('labourers'). While the former changed jobs very occasionally, the latter were frequent job-changers. The boy labourer shifts from place to place. . . . It is rare for a boy to pass through less than six places between fourteen and twenty-one, common for him to pass through twelve, while in some cases he passes through twenty or thirty. In one instance a young man of twenty-four was able to give the names and addresses of fifty employers with whom he had worked since leaving school. Moreover, the mobility of the boy labourer tends to be different in object and character from that of the boy who is learning a trade. The latter sometimes moves in order to go to a shop where a different branch of the trade is carried on, with the intention of widening his experience. . . . He may move within the trade, but he rarely moves outside it. In the case of the former . . . the main incentive to movement (apart from dismissal by the employer) is immediately higher wages, and, further, . . . the occupations through which they pass have frequently no connection with each other' – Tawney, *op. cit.*, 530.

7. B. S. Rowntree and B. Lasker, *Unemployment: A Social Study* (London: Macmillan, 1911). Previous studies of unemployment were based on statistics of applications to local Distress Committees, and later on statistics from Labour Exchanges. The difficulties of interpreting this evidence as it relates to youth unemployment are well illustrated by Chapter 5 of

S. J. Chapman and H. M. Hallsworth, *Unemployment: The Results of an Investigation made in Lancashire* (Manchester: Manchester University Press, 1909).

8. From Rowntree and Lasker, *op. cit.*, p. 12.

9. Freeman, *op. cit.* A somewhat similar methodology was later followed by E. L. Lewis, in *The Children of the Unskilled: An Economic and Social Study* (London: P. S. King & Son, 1924), which studies the careers of young people in Glasgow, Middlesbrough and Blaenau Ffestiniog. Lewis's findings suggest that the children of unskilled workers face considerable handicaps in obtaining steady skilled or semi-skilled employment, either through apprenticeship or through other means.

10. J. Jewkes and A. Winterbottom, *Juvenile Unemployment* (London: Allen & Unwin, 1933). An earlier study, of only peripheral interest, is described in *Report of an Inquiry into the Personal Circumstances and Industrial History of Boys and Girls registered for Employment* (London: HMSO, 1926).

11. Cameron, Lush and Meara, *Disinherited Youth*. See also A. J. Lush, *The Young Adult, A Report . . . under the Auspices of the Carnegie United Kingdom Trust* (Cardiff: University of Wales Press, 1941).

12. For example, in Glasgow the median wage was 10s. at fourteen, 13s. 6d. at sixteen, 20s. at eighteen, 39s. at twenty-one, and 51s. 6d. at twenty-four. In Cardiff it was 9s. 6d. at fourteen, 13s. 6d. at sixteen, 18s. at eighteen, 35s. at twenty-one and 48s. at twenty-four. In Liverpool the wages were lower than in Glasgow, but higher than in Cardiff.

13. J. Jewkes and S. Jewkes, *The Juvenile Labour Market* (London: Gollancz, 1938).

14. T. Ferguson and J. Cunnison, *The Young Wage-earner: A Study of Glasgow Boys* (London: Oxford University Press, 1951). A follow-up study – T. Ferguson and J. Cunnison, *In Their Early Twenties: A Study of Glasgow Youth* (London: Oxford University Press, 1956) – was mainly concerned with the problems of national service.

15. [M. Harris], *15 to 18: Report of the Central Advisory Council for Education – England*, vol. II (Surveys), Part 1: *The Social Survey* (London: HMSO, 1960).

16. M. P. Carter, *Home, School and Work: A Study of the Education and Employment of Young People in Britain* (Oxford: Pergamon Press, 1962). For a summary of this work, see M. P. Carter, *Education, Employment and Leisure: A Study of 'Ordinary' Young People* (Oxford: Pergamon Press, 1963).

17. J. L. Baxter, 'The Chronic Job Changer: A Study of Youth Unemployment', *Social and Economic Administration*, 9 (1975) 184–206, and 'Job Changing and Youth Unemployment', paper presented at the Conference on Youth Unemployment in Great Britain and the Federal Republic of Germany, London, Nov 1976

18. W. W. Daniel, *A National Survey of the Unemployed*, PEP Broadsheet 546 (London, 1974); and W. W. Daniel and E. Stilgoe, *Where Are They Now?: A Follow-up Study of the Unemployed*, PEP Broadsheet 572 (London, 1977).

19. Manpower Services Commission, *Young People and Work: Research Studies* (London: HMSO, 1978).

CHAPTER 3

1. The views of the classical economists are represented by works such as

A. C. Pigou, *Industrial Fluctuations* (London: Macmillan, 1927), and *The Theory of Unemployment* (London: Macmillan, 1933); and L. Robbins, *The Great Depression* (London: Macmillan, 1934). The Keynesian school is represented by A. H. Hansen, *A Guide to Keynes* (New York: McGraw-Hill, 1953), and L. R. Klein, *The Keynesian Revolution*, 2nd ed. (London: Macmillan, 1968). The modern approach may be traced back to W. H. Hutt, *The Theory of Idle Resources* (London: Cape, 1939). The Keynesian reappraisal proper begins with A. Leijonhufvud, *On Keynesian Economics and the Economics of Keynes* (New York: Oxford University Press, 1968). The modern approach reflects both Keynesian and classical influences: see, for example, R. Barro and H. Grossman, *Money, Employment and Inflation* (Cambridge: Cambridge University Press, 1976); E. Malinvaud, *Theory of Unemployment* (Oxford: Blackwell, 1977); E. S. Phelps (ed.), *Microeconomic Foundations of Employment and Inflation Theory* (London: Macmillan, 1971). Very recent work is reported in G. C. Harcourt (ed.), *The Microeconomic Foundations of Macroeconomics* (London: Macmillan, 1977), and S. Strom and L. Werin (eds), *Topics in Disequilibrium Economics* (London: Macmillan, 1978).

2. See, for example, W. J. Baumol, *Economic Theory and Operations Analysis* 4th ed. (London: Prentice-Hall, 1977), Ch. 21.

3. The actual adjustment mechanism is normally glossed over in elementary expositions of the theory. For a detailed discussion of the adjustment mechanism, see W. Hildenbrand and A. P. Kirman, *Introduction to Equilibrium Analysis* (Amsterdam: North-Holland, 1976). Another complication not considered here is that the labour supply curve may be backward bending: see, for example, R. Perlman, *Labour Theory* (New York: Wiley, 1969), Ch. 1.

4. Keynes's definition of involuntary unemployment is as follows: 'Men are involuntarily unemployed if, in the event of a small rise in the price of wage-goods relatively to the money-wage, both the aggregate supply of labour willing to work for the current money-wage and the aggregate demand for it at that wage would be greater than the existing volume of employment' – *The General Theory of Employment, Interest and Money* (London: Macmillan, 1936) p. 15.

5. See R. W. Clower, 'The Keynesian Counter-revolution: A Theoretical Appraisal', in F. H. Hahn and F. Brechling (eds), *The Theory of Interest Rates* (London: Macmillan, 1965); repr. in R. W. Clower (ed.), *Monetary Theory* (Harmondsworth: Penguin, 1969) pp. 202–11. See also Leijonhufvud, *op. cit.*, Ch. 6.

6. See E. S. Phelps, 'The New Microeconomics in Employment and Inflation Theory', and D. T. Mortensen, 'A Theory of Wage and Employment Dynamics', in Phelps (ed.), *op. cit.*, pp. 1–23 and 167–211.

7. According to Keynes, 'The contingency, which is favourable to an increase in the marginal efficiency of capital, is that in which money-wages are believed to have touched bottom, so that further changes are expected to be in the upward direction. The most unfavourable contingency is that in which money-wages are slowly sagging downwards and each reduction in wages serves to diminish confidence in the prospective maintenance of wages.... It follows, therefore, that if labour were to respond to conditions

of gradually diminishing employment by offering its services at a gradually diminishing money-wage, this would not, as a rule, have the effect of reducing real wages and might even have the effect of increasing them, through its adverse influence on the volume of output. The chief result of this policy would be to cause a great instability of prices, so violent perhaps as to make business calculations futile in an economic society functioning after the manner of that in which we live' – Keynes, *op. cit.*, pp. 265 and 269.

8. On the theory of job search, see G. J. Stigler, 'Information in Labor Markets', *Journal of Political Economy*, 70 Supplement (1962) 94–105; S. Rottenberg, 'On Choice in Labour Markets', *Industrial and Labor Relations Review*, 9 (1956) 183–99; A. Rees, 'Information Networks in Labor Markets', *American Economic Review (Papers and Proceedings)*, 56 (1966) 559–66; A. Rees and G. P. Schultz, *Workers and Wages in an Urban Labor Market* (Chicago: University of Chicago Press, 1970); and various papers in National Bureau of Economic Research, *The Measurement and Interpretation of Job Vacancies* (New York: NBER, 1966). The applications of search theory to unemployment are considered in M. W. Reder, 'The Theory of Frictional Unemployment', *Economica*, 36 (1969) 1–28; M. R. Fisher, 'The New Micro-economics of Unemployment', in Worswick (ed.), *Involuntary Unemployment*, pp. 35–57. For a dissenting view, see A. G. Hines, 'The Micro-economic Foundations of Employment and Inflation Theory: Bad Old Wine in Elegant New Bottles', *ibid.*, pp. 58–79.

9. This point is made in a more general fashion in S. Salop, 'The Noisy Monopolist: Imperfect Information, Price Dispersion and Price Discrimination', *Review of Economic Studies*, 44 (1977) 393–406.

10. For a more detailed analysis of the connection between stocks and flows among the unemployed, see R. F. Fowler, *Duration of Unemployment on the Register of Wholly Unemployed* (London: HMSO, 1968); C. Leicester, 'The Duration of Unemployment and Job Search', in Worswick, *Involuntary Unemployment*, pp. 185–202; T. F. Cripps and R. Tarling, 'An Analysis of the Duration of Male Unemployment in Great Britain, 1932–1972', *Economic Journal*, 84 (1974) 289–316; and C. C. Holt and M. H. David, 'The Concept and Measurement of Job Vacancies in a Dynamic Theory of the Labor Market', in National Bureau of Economic Research, *op. cit.*, pp. 73–110.

11. Models of the optimal duration of search are contained in J. J. McCall, 'Economics of Information and Job Search', *Quarterly Journal of Economics*, 84 (1970) 113–26; R. Gronau, 'Information and Frictional Unemployment', *American Economic Review*, 61 (1971) 290–301; and S. Salop, 'Systematic Job Search and Unemployment', *Review of Economic Studies*, 40 (1974) 225–43. An interesting paper with implications for the optimal duration of search is M. Rothschild, 'Searching for the Lowest Price When the Distribution of Prices is Unknown', *Journal of Political Economy*, 82 (1974) 689–712.

12. The difficulties of adjusting expectations are considered in A. A. Alchian, 'Information Costs, Pricing, and Resource Unemployment', in Phelps, *op. cit.*, pp. 27–52.

13. For a review of the issues, see M. M. Hauser and P. Burrows, *The Economics of Unemployment Insurance* (London: Allen & Unwin, 1969) pp. 96–110;

G. Chapin, 'Unemployment Insurance, Job Search and the Demand for Leisure', *Western Economic Journal*, 9 (1971) 102–7; and H. G. Grubel, D. Maki and S. Sax, 'Real and Insurance-induced Unemployment in Canada', *Canadian Journal of Economics*, 8 (1975) 174–91.

14. This model has been extensively used to explain urban unemployment in developing countries: see M. P. Todaro, 'A Model of Labor Migration and Urban Unemployment in Less Developed Countries', *American Economic Review*, 59 (1969) 138–48.

15. On the general issues of structural unemployment, see R. G. Lipsey,'Structural and Demand-deficient Unemployment Reconsidered', in A. M. Ross (ed.), *Employment Policy and the Labor Market* (Berkeley, Cal.: University of California Press, 1965); M. W. Reder, 'Wage Structure and Structural Unemployment', *Review of Economic Studies*, 31 (1964) 309–22; H. W. Robinson, 'The Response of Labour to Economic Incentives', in T. Wilson and P. W. S. Andrews (eds), *Oxford Studies in the Price Mechanism* (Oxford: Clarendon Press, 1951) 204–72; E. G. Gilpatrick, *Structural Unemployment and Aggregate Demand* (Baltimore: Johns Hopkins Press, 1966); and A. P. Thirlwall, 'Types of Unemployment, with Special Reference to "Non-Demand Deficient" Unemployment in the UK', *Scottish Journal of Political Economy*, 16 (1969) 20–49. For a case study of structural unemployment in a local labour market, see M. Jeffreys, *Mobility in the Labour Market* (London: Routledge & Kegan Paul, 1954).

16. The economics of training, with special reference to on-the-job training, is considered in G. S. Becker, *Human Capital* (New York: Columbia University Press, 1964); R. L. Bowlby and W. R. Schriver, 'Non-wage Benefits of Vocational Training: Employability and Mobility', *Industrial and Labor Relations Review*, 23 (1970) 500–9; H. Correa, *The Economics of Human Resources* (Amsterdam: North-Holland, 1963); H. M. Gitelman, 'An Investment Theory of Wages', *Industrial and Labor Relations Review*, 21 (1968) 323–52; D. Lees and B. Chiplin, 'The Economics of Industrial Training', *Lloyds Bank Review*, 96 (1970) 29–41; J. Mincer, 'The Distribution of Labor Incomes: A Survey with Special Reference to the Human Capital Approach', *Journal of Economic Literature*, 8 (1970) 1–26, and 'On-the-job Training: Costs, Returns and some Implications', *Journal of Political Economy*, 70 Supplement (1962) 50–79; M. Oatey, 'The Economics of Training with Respect to the Firm, *British Journal of Industrial Relations*, 8 (1970) 1–21; and W. Oi, 'Labor as a Quasi-fixed Factor', *Journal of Political Economy*, 70 (1962) 538–55.

17. On regional labour mobility and its economic determinants, see J. B. Lansing and N. Barth, *The Geographic Mobility of Labor* (Washington DC: US Government Printing Office, 1964); P. de Wolff et al., *Wages and Labour Mobility* (Paris: OECD, 1965); S. S. Bowles, 'Migration as Investment: Empirical Tests of the Human Investment Approach to Geographical Mobility', *Review of Economics and Statistics*, 52 (1970) 356–62; and R. L. Raimon, 'Interstate Migration and Wage Theory', *Review of Economics and Statistics*, 44 (1962) 428–38. The implications of regional immobility for unemployment are considered in P. C. Cheshire, *Regional Unemployment Differences in Great Britain*, (Cambridge: Cambridge University Press,

1973). The connection between housing and mobility is explored in J. B. Cullingworth, *Housing and Labour Mobility* (Paris: OECD, 1969).
18. The major works on seasonal unemployment appeared a long time ago: see, for example, S. Webb and A. Freeman (eds), *Seasonal Trades* (London: London School of Economics, 1912); and C. Saunders, *Seasonal Variations in Employment* (London: Longmans, Green, 1936).
19. On casual unemployment, see M. W. Reder, 'Theory of Occupational Wage Differentials', *American Economic Review*, 45 (1955) 833–52; and L. H. Fisher, *The Harvest Labor Market in California* (Cambridge, Mass.: Harvard University Press, 1953).
20. On the theory of screening see 'Symposium: The Economics of Information', *Quarterly Journal of Economics*, 90 (1976) 591–666.

CHAPTER 4

1. For general theories of youth unemployment, see D. N. Ashton and D. Field, *Young Workers* (London: Hutchinson, 1976); E. E. Cohen and L. Kapp (eds), *Manpower Policies for Youth* (New York: Columbia University Press, 1966); B. Duncan, 'Dropouts and the Unemployed', *Journal of Political Economy*, 73 (1965) 121–34; H. Folk, *The Problem of Youth Unemployment in the Transition from School to Work* (Princeton NJ: Princeton University Press, 1968); T. Gavett *et al.*, *Youth Unemployment and Minimum Wages* (Washington DC: US Government Printing Office, 1970); F. Kalachek, *The Youth Labor Market* (Ann Arbor, Mich: Institute of Labor and Industrial Relations, 1969); and Organisation for Economic Co-operation and Development, *Entry of Young People into Working Life* (Paris, 1977), and *Age and Employment* (Paris, 1963). Of peripheral interest are N. Bosanquet and P. Doeringer, 'Is There a Dual Labour Market in Great Britain?', *Economic Journal*, 83 (1973) 421–35; M. Roberts, 'Some Factors Affecting the Employment and Earnings of Disadvantaged Youths', *Industrial and Labor Relations Review*, 25 (1972) 376–82; and M. D. Ornstein, *Entry into the American Labor Force* (New York: Academic Press, 1976).
2. On the problems of entering work, see P. Brannen (ed.), *Entering the World of Work: Some Sociological Perspectives* (London: Department of Employment, 1975); National Youth Employment Council, *Unqualified Untrained and Unemployed* (London: HMSO, 1974); J. Maizels, 'The Entry of School Leavers into Employment', *British Journal of Industrial Relations*, 3 (1965) 77–89, and 'Changes in Employment among School Leavers: A Sample Study of One Cohort of Secondary Modern Boys', *British Journal of Industrial Relations*, 5 (1967) 211–21; B. G. Reubens, *Bridges to Work: International Comparisons of Transition Services* (London: Martin Robertson, 1977); and P. Willis, *Learning to Labour: How Working Class Kids get Working Class Jobs* (Farnborough, Hants: Saxon House, 1977). The relevant literature on occupational choice includes S. White, 'The Process of Occupational Choice', *British Journal of Industrial Relations*, 6 (1968) 166–84; and W. M. Williams (ed.), *Occupational Choice* (London: Allen & Unwin, 1974). For a rather overambitious attempt to measure the impact of

the non-income attributes of jobs on occupational choice, see D. S. Hamermesh, 'Economic Aspects of Job Satisfaction' in O. C. Ashenfelter and W. E. Oates (eds), *Essays in Labor Market Analysis in Memory of Yochanan Peter Comay* (New York: Halsted Press, 1977) pp. 53–72. For details of graduates' experience of entry into working life, see J. A. Davis, *Undergraduate Career Decisions: Correlates of Occupational Choice* (Chicago: Aldine, 1965); R. B. Freeman, *The Market for College-Trained Manpower*, (Cambridge, Mass.: Harvard University Press, 1971); *Graduate Employment, A Sample Survey* (London: PEP and Allen & Unwin, 1956); and 'Early Careers of Graduates Survey' and 'Career Attitudes of Undergraduates', *Department of Employment Gazette*, 85 (1977) 947–8 and 1083–92.

3. See, for instance, Brannen, *op. cit.*
4. The role of age qualifications in advertised vacancies is considered in J. Jolly, A. Mingay and S. Creigh, 'Age Qualifications in Job Vacancies', *Department of Employment Gazette*, 86 (1978) 166–72.
5. The evidence on the relationship between quits and the level of economic activity is largely confined to the United States: see D. S. Hamermesh, 'A Disaggregative Econometric Model of Gross Changes in Employment', *Yale Economic Essays*, (1969) 107–46; D. O. Parsons, 'Quit Rates over Time: A Search and Information Approach', *American Economic Review*, 63 (1973) 390–401, and 'Models of Labour Market Turnover: A Theoretical and Empirical Survey', in R. G. Ehrenberg (ed.), *Research in Labor Economics*, vol. I (Greenwich, Conn.: Jai Press, 1977) pp. 185–223, esp. pp. 210–13; and J. H. Pencavel, *An Analysis of the Quit Rate in American Manufacturing Industry* (Princeton, NJ: Princeton University Press, 1970).
6. The classic reference is M. W. Reder, 'Wage Structure and Structural Unemployment', *Review of Economic Studies*, 31 (1964), 309–22.

CHAPTER 5

1. See Eurostat, *Social Statistics*, no. 1, 1975, pp. 207–10, and *Labour Force Sample Survey* (Luxembourg, 1976) pp. 193–7.
2. This means that it is unnecessary to test for significant differences between sample statistics using tests such as chi-square; if the percentages are different to two significant places, they are almost certainly significantly different in the statistical sense. The use of the word 'significant' in this chapter is reserved for differences where the order of magnitude is sufficiently great to be important for policy purposes.
3. In this case both distributions are exponential. For further details see, for example, D. R. Cox and M. D. Miller, *Theory of Stochastic Processes* (London: Chapman & Hall, 1977).
4. See recent issues of the *Department of Employment Gazette*.
5. See, for example, Eurostat, *Labour Force Sample Survey* (1976) Table V. 2

CHAPTER 6

1. See Office of Population Censuses and Surveys, *General Household Survey 1973* (London: HMSO, 1975), Table 3.6; also the *General Household Survey 1975*, Table 5.7.
2. See for instance, A. J. H. Dean, 'Unemployment among School Leavers: An Analysis of the Problem', *National Institute Economic Review*, 78 (November 1976) 63–8.
3. See, for example, Eurostat, *Industrial Short-term Trends* (Luxembourg), various issues.
4. See the quarterly statistics published in the *Department of Employment Gazette*.
5. On apprenticeship and training generally, see K. Liepmann, *Apprenticeship* (London: Routledge & Kegan Paul, 1960); E. Venables, *The Young Worker at College* (London: Faber & Faber, 1967), and *Apprentices out of Their Time* (London: Faber & Faber, 1974); and G. Williams, *Recruitment to Skilled Trades* (London: Routledge & Kegan Paul, 1957). On the construction industry in particular, see G. Thomas, *Operatives in the Building Industry* (London: HMSO, 1967).
6. The quality of training in the distributive trades – and in particular in retailing – has long given cause for concern; see, for example, Select Committee on Shop Assistnts, *Report*, vols i–iii (London: HMSO, 1931). A recent survey of the distributive trades reported that over half the firms sampled experienced difficulties with recruitment and with labour matters in general; 42 per cent of recruits left before completing one year's employment – 'Survey of Manpower Resources in the Distributive Trades', *Department of Employment Gazette*, 82 (1974) 4–5.
7. See, for example, N. Bosanquet, 'The Real Low Pay Problem', and F. Field and S. Winyard, 'Low Pay in Public Employment and the Wages Council Sector', in F. Field (ed.), *Low Pay*, (London: Arrow, 1973) pp. 17–60; and 'Labour Costs in the Distributive Trades, Insurance and Banking in Great Britain, 1974', *Department of Employment Gazette*, 84 (1976) 596–605. A major study of the retail trade is O. Robinson and J. Wallace, *Pay and Employment in Retailing* (Farnborough, Hants: Saxon House, 1975).
8. See, for example, National Economic Development Office, *Engineering Craftsmen: Shortages and Related Problems* (London, 1977); Engineering Industries Training Board, *The Craftsmen in Engineering: An Interim Report* (London, 1975); and 'Work Organisation and Attitudes in Garage Workshops – Replanning for the 1980's', *Department of Employment Gazette*, 85 (1977) 951–3.
9. The shift in the unemployment – vacancies relationship in 1966 was pointed out by J. K. Bowers, P. C. Cheshire and A. E. Webb in 'The Change in the Relationship between Unemployment and Earnings Increases', *National Institute Economic Review*, 54 (1970) 44–63, and by D. Gujarati in 'The Behaviour of Unemployment and Unfilled Vacancies: Great Britain, 1958–71', *Economic Journal*, 82 (1972) 195–204. Gujarati's conjecture that the shift is the effect of higher unemployment benefit is supported by the econometric work of D. R. Maki and Z. A. Spindler, 'The Effect of Unemployment Compensation on the Rate of Unemployment in Great

Britain', *Oxford Economic Papers*, 27 (1975) 440–54. The 'dishoarding' hypothesis is expounded by J. Taylor in 'The Behaviour of Unemployment and Unfilled Vacancies: Great Britain, 1951–71: An Alternative View', *Economic Journal*, 82 (1972) 1352–65. A possible explanation of dishoarding in terms of a desire to improve the average utilisation of labour is developed in K. G. Knight and R. A. Wilson, 'Labour Hoarding, Employment and Unemployment in British Manufacturing Industry', *Applied Economics*, 6 (1974) 303–10. Another explanation, based on demographic changes in the labour force, is suggested in J. I. Foster, 'The Relationship between Unemployment and Vacancies in Great Britain (1958–72): Some Further Evidence', in D. Laidler and D. Purdy (eds), *Inflation and Labour Markets* (Manchester: Manchester University Press, 1974) pp. 164–96.

The introduction of redundancy payments does not seem to have had any direct effect on the duration of unemployment: see S. R. Parker, C. G. Thomas, N. D. Ellis and W. E. J. McCarthy, *Effects of the Redundancy Payments Act* (London: HMSO, 1971). This result is confirmed by two other surveys, which do however indicate some effect owing to unemployment benefit: see Daniel, *National Survey of the Unemployed*, Ch. 11; and D. I. MacKay and G. L. Reid, 'Redundancy, Unemployment and Manpower Policy', *Economic Journal*, 82 (1972) 1256–72.

There is a useful survey of the issues in 'The Changed Relationship between Unemployment and Vacancies', *Department of Employment Gazette*, 84 (1976), 1093–9. For a survey of US experience, see 'The Economics of Unemployment Insurance: A Symposium', *Industrial and Labour Relations Review*, 30 (1977) 431–526.

10. The UK system of social-security benefits is very complex (indeed, the difficulties of claimants in understanding it is sometimes advanced as a reason why it may have little effect on economic incentives). Some worked examples are given in J. A. Kay and M. King, *The British Tax System* (Oxford: Oxford University Press, 1978), Ch. 7.

11. However, evidence from the United States tends to support this hypothesis. In the major study by W. G. Bowen and T. A. Finegan, *The Economics of Labor Force Participation* (Princeton, NJ: Princeton University Press, 1969), the regression coefficient of the activity rate (percentage labour-force participation) on the unemployment rate is smaller for young males than it is for married women. The regression coefficient of the school enrolment rate for young males is about the same as the regression coefficient of the activity rate for young married women (see pp. 181 and 451). Because of data limitations there are no comparable results for the UK; see B. A. Corry and J. A. Roberts, 'Activity Rates and Unemployment: The UK Experience: Some Further Results', *Applied Economics*, 6 (1974) 1–21.

12. Recent trends in the number of pupils staying on into the sixth form are reviewed in 'Young People Leaving School in England and Wales' and 'Young People Leaving School in Scotland and Great Britain', *Department of Employment Gazette*, 85 (1977) 353–8 and 600–2.

13. For an analysis of trends in female labour-force participation, see Bowen and Finegan, *op. cit.*, A. Myrdal and V. Klein, *Women's Two Roles*, 2nd ed. (London: Routledge & Kegan Paul, 1968); National Manpower Council,

Womanpower (New York: Columbia University Press, 1959), Ch. 4, and *Work in the Lives of Married Women* (New York: Columbia University Press, 1958); G. G. Cain, *Married Women in the Labor Force: An Economic Analysis* (Chicago: University of Chicago Press, 1966); J. Mincer, 'Labor Force Participation of Married Women', in National Bureau of Economic Research, *Aspects of Labour Economics* (Princeton, NJ: Princeton University Press, 1962); Department of Employment, *Women and Work: A Statistical Survey* (London: HMSO, 1974); Department of Employment, *Women and Work: Sex Differences and Society* (London: HMSO, 1974); and J. A. Sweet, *Women in the Labor Force* (New York: Academic Press, 1973).

14. One of the few studies of redundancy practices at the industry level is A. D. Smith, *Redundancy Practices in Four Industries*, (Paris: OECD, 1966). It is a comparison of redundancy practices in the railway, steel, cotton and telecommunications industries of the United Kingdom and United States. It focuses mainly on written agreements and official codes of practice, rather than informal policies. Both age and seniority figure in the agreements, but mainly in connection with the terms of redundancy payments. The impact of redundancy practices on young people is not explicitly considered. The study by Parker *et al.* (*Effects of the Redundancy Payments Act*) has little to say about redundancy practices as such.

15. See the *General Household Survey, Introductory Report* (London: HMSO, 1973) Table 6.7, and *General Household Survey 1975*, Table 5.3.

16. The US literature focuses on the consequences of a combination of increased supply and downward wage rigidity owing to statutory minimum wages: see S. E. Baldwin, 'The Effect of Fixed-Wage Rises on Discriminated-against Minorities: Comment', *Industrial and Labor Relations Review*, 21 (1967) 581–2; Y. Brozen and M. Friedman, *The Minimum Wage Rate: Who Really Pays?* (Washington, DC: Free Society Association, 1966); T. Gavett *et al.*, *Youth Unemployment and Minimum Wages*; J. J. Kaufman and T. G. Foran, 'The Minimum Wage Rate and Poverty', in S. A. Levitan, W. J. Cohen and R. J. Lampman, *Towards Freedom from Want* (Madison, Wis Industrial Research Association, 1968) pp. 189–218; J. M. Peterson, 'Employment Effects of Minimum Wages 1938–1950', *Journal of Political Economy*, 65 (1957) 412–30; J. M. Peterson and C. T. Stewart, Jr, *Employment Effects of Minimum Wages* (Washington, DC: American Enterprise Institute, 1969); J. L. Simon, 'The Effects of Fixed-Wage Rises on Discriminated-against Minorities', *Industrial and Labor Relations Review*, 21 (1967) 96–7; and G. J. Stigler, 'The Economics of Minimum Wage Legislation', *American Economic Review*, 36 (1946) 358–67. Similar effects may be produced by unionisation of youth labour, although in practice this does not seem to be significant in Europe. See W. J. Goode, 'The Protection of the Inept', *American Sociological Review*, 32 (1967) 5–19; G. E. Johnson and K. C. Youmans, 'Union Relative Wage Effects by Age and Education', *Industrial and Labor Relations Review*, 24 (1971) 171–9; and A. Rees, 'Some Non-wage Aspects of Collective Bargaining', in P. D. Bradley (ed.), *The Public Stake in Union Power* (Charlottesville: University of Virginia Press, 1959) pp. 124–43.

CHAPTER 7

1. The multiplier effect is explained in detail in R. G. Lipsey, *Introduction to Positive Economics*, 4th ed. (London: Weidenfeld & Nicolson, 1975), Ch. 36.
2. This argument is sometimes expressed in terms of a 'vertical Phillips curve' centred on the 'natural rate of unemployment'.
3. See, for instance, Lipsey, *op. cit.*, Ch. 40. The proposition remains valid in an open economy (i.e. one trading with the rest of the world) provided that the import content of public-sector output is negligible; otherwise the result must be modified.
4. The problem is not that the output is produced under public ownership, but that it is not marketed. As a result people do not receive the output in direct proportion to their contribution to financing it. Some goods (for instance, national defence) are almost impossible to market, but others are not marketed even where they could be. However, even if public output is quite valueless, higher taxes may actually increase the supply of labour if the 'income effect' outweighs the 'substitution effect' (see Perlman, *Labor Theory*, Ch. 1). Thus higher taxes are not always a disincentive to the supply of labour.
5. The elasticity of demand for labour is the percentage increase in the demand for labour per unit percentage decrease in the real wage.
6. See, for instances, Jewkes and Jewkes, *The Juvenile Labour Market*, on the experience of voluntary training in the 1930s.
7. Prewar policies in a number of countries are described in International Labour Conference, *Unemployment among Young Persons* (Geneva: ILO, 1935). For an appraisal of certain aspects of UK policy, see Cameron, Lush and Meara, *Disinherited Youth*, and Morgan, *Needs of Youth*.
8. See 'MSC Evaluates Job Creation', *Department of Employment Gazette*, 85 (1977) 211–17.
9. See ibid., 696.
10. See 'Youth Employment Subsidy – Some Survey Results', *Department of Employment Gazette*, 86 (1978) 424–5.
11. See R. Lasko, 'The Work Experience Programme', ibid., 294–7.
12. See, for instance, Jewkes and Winterbottom, *Juvenile Unemployment*
13. See Organization for Economic Co-operation and Development, *The 1974–1975 Recession and Employment of Women* (Paris, 1977).
14. See G. Ashton, 'Employment and Examination Success of Day Release Students by Size of Firm', *British Journal of Industrial Relations*, 3 (1965) 89–94.

Index